# BEHAVIOR THERAPY: A CLINICAL INTRODUCTION

**Richard I. Lanyon**
Arizona State University

and

**Barbara P. Lanyon**
Psychological Counseling Services
Scottsdale, Arizona

**ADDISON-WESLEY PUBLISHING COMPANY**

Reading, Massachusetts
Menlo Park, California
London • Amsterdam
Don Mills, Ontario • Sydney

616 .8914 L296b c. 1

Lanyon, Richard I., 1937–

Behavior therapy, a clinical introduction /

This book is in the
ADDISON-WESLEY SERIES
IN CLINICAL AND
PROFESSIONAL PSYCHOLOGY

Leonard D. Goodstein
Series Editor

Copyright © 1978 by Addison-Wesley Publishing Company, Inc. Philippines copyright 1978 by Addison-Wesley Publishing Company, Inc.

All rights reserved. No part of this publication may be reproduced, stored in a retrieval system, or transmitted, in any form or by any means, electronic, mechanical, photocopying, recording, or otherwise, without the prior written permission of the publisher. Printed in the United States of America. Published simultaneously in Canada. Library of Congress Catalog Card No. 77-83022.

ISBN 0-201-04100-6
BCDEFGHIJ-DO-79

# Foreword

Clinical psychology is a rapidly expanding area of inquiry and practice. Traditional lines between clinical and other subdisciplines of psychology are rapidly eroding. Research in information processing has direct impact upon behavior therapy, work in physiological psychology affects our work in biofeedback, community psychologists need to keep abreast of what is happening in social psychology, and so on. At the same time, clinical psychologists are being called upon to work in a variety of new settings, and to continually develop new skills as well as to utilize their existing skills. Health Maintenance organizations (HMOs) ask clinical psychologists not only to provide direct clinical service to clients but also to help change the health-related behaviors of clients who do not require direct service. Community mental health centers ask their clinicians to provide direct service and to assist in developing prevention programs and program evaluation procedures. These are but a few examples of how the field of clinical psychology is expanding.

It is difficult for the professional practitioner as well as the student of clinical psychology to keep in touch with what is happening in the field. Traditional textbooks can give only superficial coverage to these recent changes and the journal literature does not provide a broad overview. The Addison-Wesley Series in Clinical and Professional Psychology is an effort to fill this gap. Taken as a whole, the series could be used as an introduction to the field of clinical psychology. A subset of these books, such as those on therapy, for example, could serve as a text for a course in therapy. Single volumes can be used for seminars when supplemented by journal articles, or as supplemental texts for courses in which the instructor feels the text is lacking in coverage of that area, or for short courses for the active professional. We hope that each of these volumes, written or edited by experts in the area, will also serve as an up-to-date overview of that area for the interested professional who feels in need of updating.

In this volume Richard I. and Barbara P. Lanyon have provided us with a fairly comprehensive overview of the newest of the psychotherapies—behavior therapy. Their volume is unique in that it skillfully interweaves theoretical principles with case illustrations. The case study presented in detail is unusual both in its completeness and in the range of behavioral management principles which it illustrates.

Webster defines a *primer* as "a small introductory volume on a subject." The Lanyons have provided exactly such a text on behavior therapy.

Leonard D. Goodstein

# Preface

For some time we have seen the need for a book that presents a structured introduction to the principles of behavior therapy within the context of actual practice. We have also wanted to write down a formal account of clinical behavior therapy procedures in the way that we use them. The invitation to prepare this book has provided us with the opportunity to address both of these needs. The book is designed for two kinds of readers: undergraduates in psychology who wish to gain a broad knowledge of the field of behavior therapy and to understand what is involved in its practice; and professional persons in training or in practice who wish to read a practical introduction to behavior therapy in order to test their interest in further study.

In writing the book we have tried to combine three goals which normally are not particularly compatible. First, we have wanted to maintain a rigorous attitude, adhering to well-defined terms and not straying in our language from the mainstream of contemporary behavioral psychology. Second, we have tried to capture and maintain the reader's interest by the free use of case materials in order to bring the principles and techniques to life. Third, and of great concern to us, we have tried to convey throughout this material the flavor of behavior therapy as actually practiced: its knowledge base and formal technology, the degree of accuracy and confidence the therapist can expect in planning strategies and attempting to carry them out, the extent of its success, and its mistakes, surprises, and frustrations. All case illustrations are based on actual examples from the authors' experience, except for necessary changes to preserve complete anonymity. The chapter-length case presented in Chapter 3 is reported accurately and is reproduced with permission of the patient and her husband.

While we believe that the book is accurate and up-to-date in its portrayal of the current state of the research literature in behavior therapy, we have made no attempt to write a research-oriented book. Researchers and writers in behavior therapy whose work has been specifically discussed are identified in the appropriate part of the text, and formal references are given at the end of the book.

The text is organized as follows. Chapters 1 and 2 provide a basic orientation to behavioral psychology and its application to therapeutic change, as well as an introduction to the work of the behavior therapist and a structured review of the process of designing and implementing strategies for change. Chapter 3 contains a detailed account of a single case, illustrating the principles and procedures outlined in the first two chapters. Chapters 4 through 9 review the behavioral formulation and treatment of a wide variety of clinical problems. Chapter 4 deals with the common difficulties of anxiety, depression, and psycho-physiological disorders, and Chapter 5 discusses the treatment of interpersonal difficulties. The application of behavior change principles to sexual problems is discussed in Chapter 6, and self-management in Chapter 7. Chapters 8 and 9 review the behavior therapist's work as a consultant: on children's problems, and in developing behavior change programs on an institutional basis.

The authors have profited from opportunities to organize and present earlier drafts of this material in a number of formal and informal teaching situations, including the Lindemann Mental Health Center, Boston, the Brookline Mental Health Center, the Boston VA Hospital, and Arizona State University. We are grateful to our colleagues and students in these settings for providing the stimulation for us to continually examine our ideas and techniques, and for giving us specific feedback in a great many areas.

Phoenix, Arizona  R. I. L.
December 1977  B. P. L.

# Contents

# 1
## What Is Behavior Therapy?  1

What is behavior?  3
Behavioral assessment  9
Observation and record-keeping  14

# 2
## Behavioral Treatment in Outline  22

Assessing patient resources  24
Designing the treatment strategy  27
Promoting effective learning  30
Procedures for new learning  32
Application to case examples  42
Concluding comment  46

# 3
# Behavior Therapy Applied: The Case of Mrs. Fisher  47

Background information  48
Initial formulation  51
Treatment procedures  52

# 4
# Common Clinical Problems  66

Anxiety  67
Treatment of anxiety  70
Treating cognitive difficulties  77
Physical and psychosomatic problems  78
Biofeedback  81
Depression  82

# 5
# Interpersonal Effectiveness  87

Assertiveness  88
Social skills training  94
Impulsive acting-out  101
Alcoholism  103

# 6
# Sexual and Marital Problems  106

Common sexual difficulties  107
Homosexuality  112

Deviant sexual behaviors 115
Marital problems 120

# Managing Your Own Behavior 126

What is self-management? 127
Behavior change strategies 128
Self-management of depression 136
Self-management and chronic pain 137
Self-management and natural childbirth 139

# Children: Parent and Teacher Consultation 141

Adult problems and children's problems 142
Working with parents and children 145
Contingency contracting 156
Individual problems in the classroom 157
Working directly with children 158
Aversive procedures 159

# Systems and Institutions 161

Psychiatric hospitals 161
Community mental health centers 166
Mental retardation 167
Juvenile delinquency 172
Behavior change systems in the classroom 176

## Epilogue 179

Provision of mental health services 180
Common criticisms of behavior therapy 180
Behavior change for the consumer 183

## References 185

## Index 189

# 1
# What Is Behavior Therapy?

Behavior therapy is a modern approach to the solution of psychological problems and difficulties. It is one of a number of psychological therapies that have been developed in the past ten or twenty years. Prior to that time, the major psychological treatment available was analytic or dynamic psychotherapy, based on the principles discovered by Sigmund Freud. Another widely used form of psychological counseling, developed in the 1940's by Carl Rogers, was client-centered, or nondirective, therapy. If a problem could not be managed by either of these two approaches, there was usually little else that could be done.

In contrast, today's public is confronted with a bewildering variety of therapists and therapies. Included are transactional analysis, gestalt therapy, encounter groups and workshops,

EST, Silva Mind Control, primal therapy, and bioenergetics. While some of these procedures merit serious consideration, many of them appear to be more or less popular fads that will be replaced in a few years by a new set.

Behavior therapy differs from most other new therapies in two basic ways. First and most important, it involves the natural development of practical procedures for alleviating human problems based on theory and research in the behavioral sciences. It represents an orderly growth of useful practical procedures based on the knowledge that research psychologists have been accumulating for most of the twentieth century. Interestingly, the rapid development of this knowledge into therapeutic procedures has taken place almost entirely since the 1960's. Within that time, more than 5000 articles have appeared in scholarly and professional journals, reporting, testing, and evaluating these procedures. This material is now the subject matter of some two dozen major textbooks, and the total number of books currently available on some aspect of behavior therapy numbers well over 200.

This, then, is the most important way in which behavior therapy differs from other new and popular therapies. Behavior therapy has a stable and comprehensive knowledge base within the mainstream of psychology and the social sciences. It shares this characteristic with other applied sciences such as engineering, architecture, and the different branches of medicine. When training to learn the skills of behavior therapy or any other applied science, the student first studies in depth the knowledge base upon which the application is founded.

The second fundamental difference between behavior therapy and most other new therapies can also be seen by examining other professions that involve application of the sciences. The relationship between the professional person and the client is collaborative; it is a consulting relationship, a teacher-student relationship, a contractual relationship. The client has a specific task to be done and the professional person is an expert in the technology needed to do it. The professional person begins by assessing the client's need, develops an estimate of the time, resources, and effort needed to achieve the goals, and then makes a straightforward proposal based on this estimate. If the proposal is acceptable, the client enters into a contractual relationship with the professional person. The contract could involve an agreement to build a house, to deliver a baby, to fit the client with contact lenses, to remove a phobia, or whatever other goal the client might wish to achieve. Behavior therapists enter into the same kind of contractual relationship with their clients as do other professionals, for the purpose of getting a specific job done.

## What Is Behavior?

What is behavior? Why are the professional psychologists who use applied behavioral science to solve their clients' personal difficulties called *behavior* therapists? A full answer to this question would require a detailed knowledge of the history of psychology. Let us simply say that by behavior we mean *definable human events*. This includes publicly observable events, such as moving about, talking, sleeping, eating—anything that a person can be observed to do. It also includes "internal" or "covert" events, which are just as real to us but cannot be publicly observed. Covert events may be classified into two distinct groups: *thoughts* and *feelings*. We shall have more to say later about the way in which thoughts and feelings appear to follow some of the same psychological principles as events that can be publicly observed.

We have just said that most behavioral psychologists define behavior to include observable events and also thoughts and feelings. This comprehensive definition of behavior reflects the fact that behavior therapy is applicable to a broad range of human difficulties, including complex problems.

There is a basic principle of behavior that should be thoroughly understood. This principle has been known for thousands of years and has been described in many different ways. Scientifically it is known as the principle of *determinism*. It states that all behaviors have causes, that nothing happens without a cause. Most people accept the principle of determinism as common sense. However, some people are offended by it, perhaps because it appears to contradict the belief that one is always able at any time to exercise "free will" in making a decision or choosing a course of action, despite past learning or current circumstances. Existential philosophy is consistent with this nondeterministic position. Nevertheless, most of today's psychologists and other scientists are convinced that human behavior is deterministic. The applied science of behavior therapy is built firmly upon the deterministic view that all behavior has causes, and upon the applied technology of behavior change that is derived from basic psychological research.

We have stated that the principles of behavior apply to all human events, that behavior can be rationally understood through these principles, and that the behavior therapist is an expert in understanding behavior and changing it. The specific ways in which human problem behaviors are understood and changed by behavior therapists is the topic for this book as a whole.

We now introduce another fundamental principle of behavior, one that addresses the question of *why* people do what they do. This principle states that, in general, behaviors are *cued* and *maintained*. By saying that behaviors are *cued*, we mean that everything we do is triggered by something else (referred to as a *stimulus*). A common example of this principle is that *eating* is often triggered by the sight of food. For some individuals, eating may be triggered by anxiety, which is an internal cue or stimulus. As another example, a normal cue for sexual arousal is an interaction with an attractive member of the opposite sex. However, if a man were sexually aroused by the sight of a young child or by wearing women's clothes, this arousal would constitute a problem for him. Another example of a problem behavior would be the patient who regularly experienced feelings of rage (an internal or covert behavior) at the sight of his father.

In addition to being cued, behavior must also be *maintained*. This statement expresses what is perhaps the oldest behavioral principle known to man. Originally it was known as the principle of hedonism, and it was restated by Sigmund Freud as the pleasure principle. Behavioral psychologists call it the *principle of reinforcement*, and state it as follows: People tend to do more frequently whatever has brought them pleasure, or positive consequences, in the past. Conversely, they tend to do less frequently whatever has brought them pain, or negative consequences, in the past. Applied to the present context, this principle reflects the fact that behaviors we perform frequently are probably being followed by pleasant consequences. Thus, if we wish to increase a behavior, we arrange to have it maintained by pleasant consequences; that is, we positively reinforce it. To illustrate, mothers tend to require their children to eat their vegetables before they can have dessert. In this example, the dessert serves as the reinforcer to increase the desired behavior of eating vegetables. Perhaps more relevant for the student, you can systematically increase your study time by rewarding yourself with a telephone call to your girlfriend or boyfriend after you have studied for a prearranged length of time.

The fact that the principles of behavior are not confined to observable actions but also apply to thoughts and feelings is one of the more interesting and important recent discoveries of behavioral scientists. A significant aspect of social development in children is their ability to learn specific thoughts. For example, we teach children to respond to the cue of the roadside curb by thinking the thought, "Stop, look, and listen." We further teach them to use this thought as a cue for the overt behavior of stopping, looking, and listening. The whole sequence of behaviors is reinforced immediately by parental approval. The eventual reinforcement, of course, is one's physical safety, but people need immediate reinforcement in order to learn new behaviors.

Why teach the internal cue at all? Because it can be rehearsed and reinforced in the classroom and at home, in the absence of a curb and traffic. In the above example, a thought served as a cue for an overt behavior. Because the same principles tend to apply to thoughts and feelings as to overt behaviors, any one of these three can serve as a cue. Thus, for some people a feeling (such as anger) may trigger an overt behavior (such as a physical assault). To take our reasoning yet further, a thought or a feeling can serve as a reinforcer to maintain a behavior in the same way as an overt act. Thoughts about loved ones make you feel good, and you think about them more often. Thoughts about death make most people feel anxious, and we therefore tend to think about death much less frequently than would be expected in view of the number of death cues that are present in our everyday environment.

Let us reemphasize what has just been said. An event or action (which could be a thought, a feeling, or an overt behavior) is triggered by a cue (which could be a thought, a feeling, or an overt behavior) and is maintained or reinforced by its consequences (which could be a thought, a feeling, or an overt behavior).

The basic principles of behavior tend to oversimplify what actually happens in real life. Sometimes it is very difficult to discover what reinforcers are maintaining a particular behavior, especially if the behavior is something that the person has been doing habitually for many years. Research psychologists have added many exceptions and wrinkles to these basic principles, and the behavior therapist will find it necessary to develop a fair amount of sophistication before being able to utilize them productively to help people with personal problems. Such sophistication can be developed only by practice at utilizing the technology of behavior change while keeping in mind both the basic principles and the practical changes that are needed.

## What Is a Problem?

Let us now examine some real-life problems to see how they would be viewed according to the principles we have just presented. Basically, problems are of two kinds. The first kind is present when the frequency of a behavior is not appropriate; that is, either too great or too small. Obesity, for example, involves too much eating. Insomnia involves too little sleep. A person with a chronic anxiety problem has too much anxiety. The common problem of shyness is a double-barreled one: too much social anxiety and too little social interaction. Each of these components of shyness tends to maintain the other. In other words, social interaction triggers anxiety, to which shy people respond by decreasing their frequency of social interaction still further.

The second type of problem is present when the frequency of the behavior is appropriate, but occurs at the wrong time and place. That is, the behavior is triggered by the wrong cues. The child who wets the bed, for example, urinates at the wrong time and place. He must instead learn to respond to the cues of a full bladder by getting up and going to the bathroom. Another example would be the sexual exhibitionist, who engages in sexual behavior in public rather than in private. This type of problem is also present in the person who displays anger at inappropriate times.

Most real-life personal problems for which people seek professional therapy tend to be more complicated than the simple examples we have given. Problems have a way of causing further problems, and a person's several different problems may become intertwined in a complex and confusing manner. It is the behavior therapist's task to sort them out and to make plans for dealing with each in an appropriate manner.

## Voluntary and Involuntary Behavior

In most of the examples that we have discussed, the problem behaviors have been voluntary in nature. Eating is voluntary; social interaction is voluntary; stopping at the roadside curb is voluntary. Some of them, however, have been involuntary, that is, they occur without deliberate plans, or even despite our plans. Thus, for most people, negative feelings are involuntary. We would much rather not feel anxious, but it happens anyway. Other behaviors that are mostly involuntary are falling asleep (or failing to do so), feelings of depression, and persistent obsessional thoughts. Sexual behavior is partly voluntary and partly involuntary. It is important to understand that exactly the same principles apply to both kinds of behavior, voluntary and involuntary. Both are triggered by specific cues (which may themselves be voluntary or involuntary), and both are maintained at their existing rate by some kind of reinforcement. A related, though not identical, way of referring to these two general kinds of behaviors would be those which are under one's immediate control, and those which are not.

The fact that voluntary and involuntary behaviors both follow behavioral principles enables the behavior therapist to successfully modify involuntary behaviors that would at first glance appear to be uncontrollable. One way to deal with insomnia, for example, would be to have the patient voluntarily arrange his sleeping environment so that it contains the greatest possible number of cues that normally trigger sleep. First, the patient must be tired; that is, his bodily state must be as ready as possible for sleep. This is most easily arranged by controlling the amount of time since his previous sleep. Other cues are darkness, a horizontal position on a bed covered with bedclothes, freedom from distracting sounds, relative freedom from worrisome thoughts, and a state of definite physical relaxation. Under these conditions, the majority of persons readily fall asleep.

## The Therapeutic Relationship

So far we have discussed the general orientation of behavior therapists and their way of viewing human behavior, both adaptive and unadaptive. It should be clear at this point that problem behavior is no different in principle from nonproblem behavior. Perhaps we can say that a particular behavior constitutes a problem if it causes distress to the person either directly or because somebody else complains about it.

We now move to a different but equally important topic: how the behavior therapist and the client agree to work together. We have already seen that the relationship between the behavior therapist and the client is the same as the relationship that any other professional person would have with a client. We emphasize this point because it has been traditional in psychotherapy for therapists or psychoanalysts to have a somewhat different relationship with their clients. In classical psychoanalysis, the analyst undertakes to perform a comprehensive analysis of all major areas of personal functioning for the client, no matter what the particular problem happens to be. This approach is based on the premise that psychological problems are generally the result of deep-rooted disorders of personality. In psychoanalytic theory, such disorders are believed to originate from particular difficulties experienced during early childhood, and it is further believed that these childhood causes must be uncovered and analysed in detail in order for proper personality development to occur. Thus, the major focus of the traditional psychoanalyst is on the patient's childhood, regardless of the problem. The analyst encourages the patient to develop a particular kind of highly dependent relationship with him called *transference*, and the transference relationship serves as an important tool in the analyst's work of uncovering the presumed childhood bases of the patient's current difficulties.

Although few therapists practice classical psychoanalysis today, many psychotherapists still rely heavily on the therapeutic transference relationship as an important tool in working with their clients. This traditional therapeutic approach is often called relationship psychotherapy in order to distinguish it from behavioral psychotherapy.

Although behavior therapists do not have a transference relationship with their clients, they do indeed foster a definite kind of relationship. As stated above, it is a positive and cooperative relationship of the kind that is encouraged between any professional person and a client. The behavior therapist works to keep the client motivated to do what is required of him and to maintain the client's confidence in his ability to promote a successful outcome.

### Empathy and Understanding

No matter what the therapist's orientation, there are certain personal qualities and general clinical skills that form a foundation for the application of specific technical skills. The personal qualities to which we are referring are those that one would expect of a member of the helping professions: empathy, warmth, genuineness, understanding, and emotional maturity. With these basic qualities as a foundation, therapists develop a range of general clinical skills: how to give support and reassurance to a patient in crisis, how to react appropriately to an angry and threatening patient, how to probe for more information without stressing the patient beyond his capacity, and how to firmly and therapeutically set limits when a patient makes unrealistic demands. Many more examples could be given of these general professional skills in interacting therapeutically with troubled people. The behavior therapist must develop and utilize these skills just like any other therapist. It is not sufficient to have a knowledge of psychopathology and applied behavioral science and to know the technology of applying this knowledge. A therapist cannnot work solely from a textbook, be it behavioral, psychoanalytic, or any other. It is important to understand this point because the behavior therapist is sometimes erroneously described as not needing to have these general clinical skills. While on the topic, it is worth noting that the opposite belief is occasionally encountered, namely, the view that useful therapeutic work can be done by a therapist possessing *only* general clinical skills. While this may be true in a few cases, it is doubtful that much lasting change can be brought about unless the therapist also possesses an adequate technical knowledge of ways of solving human problems.

## Behavioral Assessment

It is a fundamental rule of behavior therapy that the therapist and client work toward explicit goals that they have agreed upon in advance. As we have already seen, the client's problem is generally formulated in terms of behaviors that need to be changed. In essence, the first question to which the behavior therapist seeks an answer from the client is "How do you want to be different?" or

"What is it about yourself that you would like to change?" A more detailed analysis of this question would lead to a number of further questions: "What behaviors would you like to increase in frequency?" "What behaviors would you like to decrease in frequency?" "What behaviors would you like to perform under different circumstances?" A problem situation where a desired behavior is not currently being performed at all is, of course, an extreme case of the need to increase the frequency of the behavior. The task of getting the behavior started in the first place requires special procedures such as modeling or shaping, topics to be discussed later.

The general topic of restating the client's difficulties using the specific concepts and language of the behavior therapist and then designing behavior change strategies to accomplish the stated goals is termed *behavioral assessment*. Behavioral assessment includes the following formal steps: (1) defining the problem in behavioral terms; (2) identifying the events that are cueing and maintaining the problem behaviors; (3) formulating an analysis of the problem situation and behavioral strategies for changing it; (4) assessing the client's resources for bringing about change; and (5) negotiating a realistic therapeutic contract with the client, based on what the therapist believes can actually be accomplished.

## Case Illustrations

In the following pages we discuss each of these steps in turn, and illustrate them with reference to three specific cases: Mrs. Osborn, a lady with an obesity problem; Mrs. Smith, whose problem involved a fear of being left alone; and Mr. Watts, who sought help because his life had lost its meaning. We begin by giving detailed attention to the first step, namely, taking the client's problem as presented and restating it in the language and framework of the behavior therapist.

### Mrs. Osborn: Obesity

Mrs. Osborn, a 34-year-old married woman with two children, was 60 pounds overweight and sought professional help after she had been unable to lose the weight on her own. At first glance this would seem to be a simple problem in decreasing the frequency of food intake. However, dieting is often more easily said than done. Also, overweight people sometimes have additional problems such as social shyness, unassertiveness, depression, or marital conflict, and these problems may interact with the overeating problem. How is the behavior therapist to know when obesity is a simple problem of overeating and when additional problem behaviors must be taken into account? The behavior therapist assumes that the problem as presented is the primary one, but in addition conducts a general psychological and behavorial inquiry in which he is especially alert to the kinds of difficulties that are often associated with the stated problem. In Mrs. Osborn's case, for example, the therapist's initial inquiries led him to suspect that there was a significant amount of marital conflict which appeared to be based on sexual difficulties. The therapist judged that in order to make more than superficial headway on the obesity, these additional problem behaviors should also be formulated in behavioral terms and changed appropriately.

How does the behavior therapist know what possible problem areas to look for in addition to the stated problem? This is partly a matter of knowledge in psychopathology and partly a matter of experience as a behavior therapist. In addition, clues to possible areas of difficulty might be obtained through psychological tests such as the Minnesota Multiphasic Personality Inventory (MMPI) and other self-report questionnaires and inventories.

The behavior therapist usually shares information fully with the client as it is obtained. The client and the behavior therapist are essentially partners sharing the task of solving the problem together. The first part of the task is to understand and agree upon the dimensions of the problem. With Mrs. Osborn, there was ready agreement on the fact that she needed to decrease her food intake. There was also some tentative agreement that marital and possibly sexual problems were involved, but at this point in the behavioral assessment procedure she was not able to supply enough information about them to permit the therapist to make even a preliminary formulation as to what behaviors should be increased, decreased, or performed under different circumstances. Thus, it was agreed that more information was needed, and it was agreed that Mrs. Osborn would ask her husband to accompany her on the second visit to the therapist. The therapist anticipated that this would result in an agreement as to which of their behaviors the Osborns should be asked to observe at home, with the object of keeping structured written records.

### Mrs. Smith: Fear of being alone

Mr. Smith, a middle-aged man, requested help for his wife, who he said was too dependent. When asked for further information, he found the problem difficult to explain. His concern, however, was his wife's insistence that he should accompany her everywhere she went. The therapist interviewed husband and wife together and verified that the husband's statement was indeed correct. In addition, either the husband or one of their children had to stay at home whenever the wife was at home. The family's attempts to leave her alone even for a short period of time were met with tears and her insistence that "something terrible would happen." There was no doubt at all that she was truly terrified of being alone. After further discussion with the couple, it was agreed that the problem had two components: the wife spent too little time alone, and her anxiety when alone was too high. Thus, the behavior therapist's task was to increase her frequency of spending time alone and to decrease her anxiety when alone. It would be plausible to assume that these two behaviors might be related, although this assumption cannot be taken for granted.

Once having agreed on the apparent problem, the therapist enlisted the couple's help in the task of gathering data in order to determine what was maintaining the wife's anxiety about being alone and what behaviors by other family members were contributing to her difficulties. It sometimes becomes apparent after gathering such information that the real problem is rather different from its initial formulation, or that further problems are involved. There will also be instances when the patient may not agree with the therapist about the nature of the problem. Illustrations of both kinds of situations are given in case examples later in the book.

The two problems we have described (obesity and fear of being alone) are fairly specific. Let us now look at a different kind of problem, one which initially might seem very difficult to view in behavioral terms.

### Mr. Watts: A problem of apathy

Mr. Watts, a successful business executive, came to the therapist complaining that life had lost its meaning. When asked to be more specific, he simply said that he really did not know. All he could say was that there seemed to be no meaning in his life and that nothing seemed to be important to him nowadays. Although he had a family and a responsible job, he felt little commitment to them. It was this lack of commitment that led him to seek help, for he had found himself seriously wondering whether he should bother going to work or even showing up at home. Although he did not understand these difficulties, he was astute enough to recognize that he had a serious problem.

The behavior therapist noted that certain behaviors which should be vital for this man—going to work, and supporting his family—were in danger of diminishing or disappearing entirely. Since the patient had not described overt behaviors, but only thoughts and feelings about lack of responsibility, not going to work, and not supporting his family, the therapist told him that it was fortunate that he had sought help while the problems were still at the stage of thinking and feeling, rather than waiting until actual changes in overt behavior had added to his difficulties.

The type of problem we have just described is sometimes referred to as an *existential dilemma*, since it raises questions about the meaning of existence for a particular person. Problems of this nature are often unsuited to behavior therapy, although some can be successfully treated behaviorally. In the present case, the therapist decided first to consider the possibility that events which were reinforcing for this man were becoming less and less frequent in his life and that few reinforcers were now available for his activities, either at work or at home. The reader should note that we are talking about the patient's *motivation* in life, and that the terms motivation and reinforcement refer to essentially the same psychological processes. In this example, it is important to understand that the behavior therapist would strongly encourage the man to remain in his current job and with his family at least until there was a better understanding of his current dissatisfactions. This strategy might be contrasted with the therapeutic approach of encouraging the patient to actively explore alternative life styles in an effort to "find himself." Most behavior therapists would believe that such action would make a satisfactory solution to the problem more difficult to achieve.

## Toward a Therapeutic Contract

Two principles are of basic importance throughout the behavior therapy process: (a) open and honest communication between therapist and patient, and (b) continual refining of the therapeutic goals as new information is obtained. Because the therapist is not yet in a position to know how long treatment will take or even how to treat the patient, a therapeutic contract cannot be developed at this time. However, the principles stated above should be applied in keeping the patient fully informed of the process of planning the therapy. Thus, the patient should be made aware that the therapist's next step will be to have the patient start gathering systematic observations to find out how the problem behaviors are being triggered and maintained. The patient should also understand that in this stage of the process, additional data might come to light that will cause the therapist to revise his view as to the most important aspects of the patient's problem. At this point it is possible to give most patients an initial opinion as to whether treatment is possible, how long it might take, and how complex and effortful it might be.

## Observation and Record-Keeping

Observations and records are the very core of the behavioral assessment process. Because the process of assessment is continued to some extent throughout the entire therapy process, observation and record-keeping also continue throughout the entire period. Once the behavior change procedures begin, assessment has two purposes: (a) to refine the formulation of the patient's problems, and (b) to evaluate the extent to which therapeutic changes have been made. In all cases, the procedures for assessment are the same. This section, however, deals specifically with the process of assessment before the beginning of treatment.

When people have problems that they are unable to deal with effectively, they tend to seek the causes. Almost universally, they ask "Why?" "Why am I anxious?" "Why am I overweight?" "Why has life passed me by?" It is natural and universal for people to look for the causes of their difficulties. In fields such as medicine, direct answers can often be found by asking "Why?" "Why is my nose running?" "Because I have a cold," or, "Because I have hay fever." In these cases it is useful to get an answer to the question "why" because the solution is often directly available. Thus, if the answer is "hay fever," modern drugs can often cure the running nose almost immediately. If the answer is "a cold," somewhat less can be done, and the treatment of choice might involve medication plus enforced rest and adequate warmth. Unfortunately, most psychological problems are rather more complex, and responses to the questions "why" almost always lead to answers that are pretty well useless. In fact, the answers often tend to be worse than useless, for they set the patient on the wrong track. "Why is life passing me by?" a spinster might ask. "Because I have no friends." "Why do I have no friends?" "Because I am not a likable person." And so she might continue her ruminations, devaluing herself and moving further away from the type of thinking that would enable her to resolve her difficulties.

If not "why," then what questions does the behavior therapist ask his patients? As we have said earlier in the chapter, he asks questions designed to find out what cues are triggering the problem behaviors and what events are maintaining or reinforcing them. In other words, the therapist and the patient together embark upon the search for the relevant events that are responsible for the problem behavior. The reason for this search is, of course, to change these events and thereby bring about new, adaptive behaviors.

It is useful to regard the collaborative work of the patient and therapist, especially in the assessment phase, as that of *behavioral detectives*. The mission is to find out what leads to what. What thoughts or feelings or overt behaviors act as cues for the problem events, and what thoughts, feelings, or overt behaviors reinforce the problem events? The cues and the reinforcers might be aspects of the patient's own behavior, or they might be aspects of somebody else's behavior, or they might be aspects of the environment that have to do with nobody in particular. The notion of the behavioral detective conveys a further important idea: that the observations should be precise, comprehensive, accurate, and as reliable as possible. The aspects of the problem behavior which the therapist trains the patient to observe can be summarized by three words: What? When? and Where?

To what extent are people capable of making accurate and reliable observations about themselves? Until quite recently, psychologists commonly believed that self-observations were so unreliable and biased as to be useless for serious work. Research-oriented behavior therapists have now successfully challenged this view, and they have been able to show that people can be trained to gather information about themselves that is both accurate and reliable. Obviously, if accurate self-observation were not possible, there would be no way to gather information about a person's private or internal events, that is, about thoughts and feelings. Self-observation is not something that comes naturally to people, but like any skill, it has to be learned.

Another important point regarding self-observation is related to the fact that people tend to avoid situations and thoughts that are anxiety-arousing. Such avoidances are maintained by anxiety reduction; in other words, people learn to avoid anxiety-arousing cues because anxiety is unpleasant. Because most psychological problems involve some degree of anxiety, people often have rather little information about the events associated with their problem. Thus, the therapist might warn the patient that a certain amount of anxiety could be generated as a result of his close and careful self-observation. One common outcome is that patients find themselves highly disinclined to do the observations even though they are normally conscientious about personal tasks in their lives.

Because the patient is the most convenient observer of his own behavior, most behavior therapists rely rather heavily on self-observations. Basically, the patient is asked to observe and write down the events that are associated with a problem event. As we have stated earlier, observations include *what* the event is, *when* it occurs, and *where* it occurs. When and where refer to things that are associated with the problem event, as will be made clear in the examples below. It should not be forgotten that covert events, that is, thoughts and feelings, are just as important to be observed as visible events. Because the patient will not know exactly what to write down, and because the therapist initially may have little idea as to where to look for the critical cues and reinforcers, the patient is usually told to begin by keeping very complete records, noting everything that takes place at the time of the problem behavior, no matter how unimportant it may seem.

## Examples of Observation and Record-keeping

Let us now look at some actual examples of observation and record-keeping. We follow up on the three patients whose problems we introduced in the previous section: Mrs. Osborn, whose problem was overweight; Mrs. Smith, who was fearful of being left alone; and Mr. Watts, whose life had lost its meaning. For each patient, we discuss the observations and records that were requested and the way in which the therapist used this information to help in formulating possible treatment strategies.

## Mrs. Osborn

In working with overweight persons, it is usual for the therapist to request rather elaborate records. The core of the record is an accurate account of every item of food that is consumed. The patient is taught to convert this record continuously to calories so that the patient has a precise total of the number of calories consumed during each day. The patient's record will also contain the usual information as described above: the time when each food item is consumed, the place where it is consumed, the presence or absence of other people, and potential covert cues (thoughts and feelings) such as hunger, loneliness, anxiety, anger, or plans for forthcoming events.

Let us now see what information was available from Mrs. Osborn's records. This particular patient had attempted to diet a number of times previously, and was quite skilled at estimating the number of calories in any given item of food. For patients who do not have this skill, a calorie-counter booklet is a necessary adjunct. Mrs. Osborn's records over two weeks showed that she consumed an average of 2200 calories per day. Surprisingly, she ate little or nothing until mid-afternoon. When questioned, she said that she would make a new resolution every morning to diet on that day, and she would then proceed by eating neither breakfast nor lunch but keeping herself busy with household chores. During the afternoon, however, she would eat a large variety of foods, including fancy breads and pastries, leftover meat from the previous day, and whatever else happened to be available. She would then eat her regular supper and continue snacking throughout the rest of the evening. By mid-evening she would develop strong feelings of guilt about breaking her diet and would resolve once again to begin on the following day.

The feelings and thoughts associated with Mrs. Osborn's afternoon eating mainly involved hunger. It would be at these times that she planned her meals and her trips to the supermarket. During the evenings her husband would frequently complain about tasks left undone in the house, her weight, and her lack of sexual interest. These complaints would generate feelings which were best described as a mixture of anger, depression, frustration, and guilt.

As illustrated in the above example, the behavior therapist utilizes the patient's records as a starting point for making a variety of inquiries to help expand upon the pool of available information and to gain a fuller understanding of the cues and reinforcers associated with the patient's difficulties. Knowing how to conduct such an inquiry is a matter of experience in both general clinical skills and the technology of behavioral assessment.

One of the most important cues for eating is the actual presence of appetizing food. It is also known that overweight people are generally more vulnerable to the attractions of the physical presence of food than people who do not have a weight problem. Further, overweight people tend to surround themselves with easily available appetizing food to a much greater extent than other persons. Thus, we should not be surprised that Mrs. Osborn had large quantities of highly attractive snacking food in the house at all times. Interestingly, Mrs. Osborn herself was initially surprised when the therapist drew this conclusion from her observational records. She then added that there were always dishes of candy in the house primarily for her husband. Further questioning showed, however, that it was Mrs. Osborn who ate it.

From these initial observational records and detailed questioning based on them, the therapist drew the following tentative conclusions. Mrs. Osborn's snacking in the afternoon seemed rather obviously to be cued by normal hunger, and an agreement was made that she would eat regular breakfast and lunch. With regard to her snacking in the evening, the therapist noted that her husband would consistently fail to recognize her positive efforts at housekeeping and would instead criticize her indiscriminately, leading her to avoid him and seek solace in food. This interaction raised the further question of whether the husband was experiencing psychological problems independent of the marital relationship. Finally, as with all obese patients, Mrs. Osborn was given a variety of instructions designed to remove as many as possible of the eating cues from her environment. For example, she was to purchase only essential foods and she was to have no food visible anywhere in the house. More detailed descriptions of the kinds of basic instructions to be given to an overweight person can be found in the Stuart and Davis book *Slim Chance in a Fat World* and in *Permanent Weight Control* by Michael and Kathryn Mahoney. We will continue with our description of Mrs. Osborn's treatment in Chapter 2.

**Mrs. Smith**
Let us next examine observation and record-keeping procedures as they apply to Mrs. Smith, whose problem involved difficulties with being alone. The therapist instructed her to keep a daily record of the times when she was actually alone (such as 4:30–5:30 P.M.) plus a brief note as to where she was at the time (e. g., at home) and whatever other events were associated with it. These could include thoughts (e. g., that my husband will never come back for me), feelings (anxiety about how to support the children), a description of how she spent the time (e. g., watching TV), and any other related information (e. g., the feelings of depression lasted for about one hour after her husband returned). It can readily be appreciated that at the first try, the patient might not write down all the information needed by the therapist. A certain amount of discipline is needed on the part of the patient in order to keep the records. Also, several weeks of "shaping" by the therapist might be required in order to teach the patient to keep the records fully and appropriately. Sometimes it is helpful for the therapist to prepare a structured record sheet or daily chart for the patient.

The examples in parentheses above represented the most common themes running through Mrs. Smith's daily records over a period of two weeks, covering about a dozen instances of being left alone. These themes gave the following information. First, her fears appeared to be related at least in part to abandonment by her husband. However, she did not experience the fear when her older children were present, even if her husband was not. Second, we see that Mrs. Smith typically engaged in a passive activity when alone, giving her plenty of opportunity to think obsessively about possible catastrophes. The therapist's questioning about her note on feelings of depression revealed that her husband would react to her depression by giving her a great deal of attention and reassurance.

These notes represent a simplified version of the work done by Mrs. Smith and the therapist, and they convey a realistic impression of the kind of information that is usually gained from the patient's self-observations. Several lines of action were followed up by the therapist. Mrs. Smith was questioned about possible origins of her fear of being left alone to support the children, and the therapist met jointly with her and her husband in order to clarify the likelihood that he would actually abandon his family. At the same time, the therapist explained to Mr. Smith that the reassurance he gave to his wife when he came home might actually be reinforcing her inactivity and depression. We will continue our discussion of Mrs. Smith's treatment in Chapter 2.

## Mr. Watts

The reader will recall that Mr. Watts' complaint was that his life had lost its meaning. Because the therapist suspected that stable reinforcers for "meaningful" life behaviors might be lacking in his environment, and because his complaints centered about thoughts and feelings, the therapist instructed him to keep records of both kinds of events. Thus, Mr. Watts was asked to keep systematic written notes of everything "pleasant" or "nice" that happened to him: verbal praise, smiles, other forms of social approval, statements about his worth, positive self-statements, gifts and presents, food and drink, satisfying activities, etc., either at home, at work, or in recreation. In short, the therapist wanted to know about all events that had any reinforcing value for him, when and where they occurred, and what other events were associated with them. In the second set of records, he was asked to note when and where thoughts of "meaninglessness" occurred. If they lasted over a period of time, he was to note the events associated with their beginning and the events associated with their disappearance.

Mr. Watts' records on the topic of "meaninglessness" seemed initially rather unhelpful. He reported that these thoughts persisted practically nonstop and involved such sentiments as despair that his job would lead to any advancement, daydreams about the type of work he was formerly involved in before his present supervisory position, thoughts about whether he could maintain his three children in college, distaste for his daughter's boyfriends, conflict with his wife who frequently pressured him to engage in neighborhood social activities in which he had no interest, and a variety of thoughts about needing a new car, meeting his family's miscellaneous demands for money, and wondering if he should change his conservative appearance with new clothes and a modern hairstyle.

The other set of records, to do with pleasurable events or reinforcers, was almost entirely blank. The only item on the list was "driving home from work." The therapist's questioning revealed that this was the only time when there were no demands upon Mr. Watts, and when he had an opportunity to relax and listen to the radio. The therapist, initially puzzled by these records, asked him to describe in detail a typical day at work, and stopped him frequently to ask for the actual words spoken to him and by him to other people. It quickly became apparent that most of Mr. Watts' workday was spent in receiving complaints from the senior management of the company and also from the first-level supervisors below him. Another aspect of his responsibility included the evaluation of personnel, reprimanding or firing those whose performance did not meet company standards.

The therapist was now able to appreciate that the record of home activities also involved the constant receiving of complaints. Indeed, the time which Mr. Watts spent driving to and from work was his only period of escape from this constant aversive stimulation. Mr. Watts, a highly intelligent, though very unassertive, man with a strong sense of responsibility, was initially surprised when this analysis of his current life circumstances was presented to him. After reflection, however, he readily agreed that it was indeed accurate.

The reader is again cautioned that careful training of a patient through several weeks of successive approximations in self-observation is usually required in order to arrive at an adequate formulation of the problem situation, based on the data from the patient's observational records and the therapist's knowledge and experience in the technology of behavior change. We have presented three typical case examples in which we have attempted to convey the sense of how a behavior therapist in practice would actually approach his patients. While applied behavioral science is obviously not as exact as chemistry or mathematics, the therapist with an actively cooperating patient is generally able to develop a formulation of the patient's problem that is accurate enough to suggest a specific approach to treatment.

# 2

# Behavioral Treatment in Outline

In Chapter 1 we introduced a definition of behavior as encompassing human events in general, including thoughts and feelings as well as publicly observable actions. We saw how behavior therapists expect their patients to be active collaborators in the task of finding out what is maintaining the unhappy or dissatisfying state of affairs and in using behavioral technology to design and implement the needed changes. We saw that the initial steps in this enterprise are to specify the problem or set of problems as precisely as possible and to try to determine what specific cues are triggering and/or reinforcing each instance of the difficulty. For this purpose, a considerable amount of accurate information is needed about the events associated with instances of the problem. The patient is trained by the therapist to become an accurate self-observer and to make detailed written records of each instance of the difficulty and the associated events. The therapist asks further questions based on these records and does his best to formulate preliminary answers as to what events are acting to cue and maintain the problem behaviors.

The stage is thus set to formulate and implement specific procedures for bringing about the desired changes. It would be convenient indeed if psychological difficulties could be classified into neat categories, each associated with a specific cause or set of causes and a specific treatment. Unfortunately this is not the case. Psychologists and psychiatrists now recognize that most psychological or mental problems are not like physical or medical problems, where certain symptom clusters indicate the existence of specific diseases with direct implications for treatment. Rather, in analyzing psychological problems, the behavior therapist must rely to a considerable degree on basic principles.

This is not meant to imply that the state of affairs is confused or chaotic, however. The behavior therapist assumes that there are lawful principles underlying the learning, cueing, and maintenance of behavior. Furthermore, once the nature of the difficulty is clearly understood and the characteristics and resources of the patient are taken into account, specific treatment techniques are often available. Although our existing practical framework for the understanding of human problems based on behavioral science is not as far advanced as our understanding of medical problems, researchers in mental health and human adjustment are continuing to make rapid strides in this endeavor.

It is worth noting that advances in the understanding of behavioral problems have probably been hindered over the years by the belief that they are exactly parallel to medical problems. Most psychologists now believe that when researchers finally achieve an ultimate and satisfactory understanding of behavioral problems and develop a sophisticated framework for evaluating and treating them, it will be rather different in nature from the medical model of diagnosis and treatment.

Despite these reservations, some useful beginnings have been made in showing that certain behavioral problems do have identifiable causes and respond to specific treatment techniques. For example, most persons with significant obesity problems have certain characteristics in common, and there are definite similarities in their treatment procedures. We have already noted some of these similarities in discussing the case of Mrs. Osborn. The pioneering work of sex researchers William Masters and Virginia Johnson has shown that sexual maladjustment is another area in which persons with specific problems, such as impotence, for example, tend to have certain causal characteristics in common and to respond to the same treatment. Research is also beginning to suggest identifiable causes and treatment procedures for behavioral problems such as obsessive-compulsive difficulties, phobias, and some aspects of depression.

## Assessing Patient Resources

It should by now be clear that the behavior therapy patient plays an active collaborative role in his own treatment. Essentially, the basic work of therapy is done by the patient under the direction of the therapist. In order to carry out these responsibilities in treatment successfully, the patient must have certain characteristics and skills. Perhaps the most important characteristic of all is a willingness to engage in the "homework" assignments that are agreed upon. Assignments are of two general kinds: (a) gathering and recording information, and (b) engaging in progressive small steps involving specific new behaviors. If a patient does not bring in comprehensive and accurate information, it will be difficult for the therapist to determine which techniques will be successful in leading to the desired changes or to monitor the patient's progress in making these changes. If the patient does not engage in the step-by-step procedures as agreed with the therapist, he will never reach the desired goals of behavior change.

In practice, most patients are willing to learn and engage in self-observation to a satisfactory degree. We have already noted that self-observation is a set of skills that can be systematically taught. However, the more work the therapist has to do in teaching these basic skills to the patient, and in checking up on him and finding ways to ensure that he does what is agreed upon, the longer the entire process of therapy will take and the more complex it will become for both the patient and therapist. The same comments apply to new behaviors on which the patient and therapist have agreed. The more completely the therapist has to spell out each step, get the patient to agree on an actual time and place to do them, and at times even call the patient to check up on him, the longer and more complex the therapy process becomes.

A second important characteristic needed by the patient is a willingness to permit the therapist to take control of some of the major and anxiety-producing aspects of his life. In other words, the patient is asked to deal slowly but directly with the distressing problems which brought him into therapy in the first place, and perhaps eventually to engage in new and feared behaviors under the careful supervision of the therapist. Because the therapist strives to accomplish the desired changes as rapidly as possible, and because patients are sometimes slow to develop a full understanding of the reasons for their difficulties, patients are often requested to do things for reasons they do not yet fully understand. The patient who insists on full understanding or "insight" before being willing to engage in step-by-step changes will prolong the time of treatment.

It is also important to understand that a person may not initially "feel" like making a particular change; however, in many instances it is much more economical to ask the patient to make the change regardless of feelings. In such cases, the patient's feelings tend to change soon after the behavior changes. For example, the person who compulsively checks every light switch a dozen times must be persuaded to refrain from this behavior even though he is convinced that it is absolutely necessary. Once the person has refrained from performing this compulsive behavior for a short time, his initial anxiety about catastrophic consequences will generally subside and he will feel more comfortable than he did while performing the behavior. It should be emphasized that the therapist designs a program in which the behavioral steps should be sufficiently small that the patient is not asked to tolerate unmanageable anxiety.

A third important resource in behavioral treatment is the availability of other people in the patient's environment whose help can be enlisted in bringing about the desired changes. In fact, when the patient's difficulties actively involve other people such as spouse and children, it is difficult or impossible to get the job done without their active collaboration. In Mrs. Osborn's case, for example, to be detailed more fully below, her husband's sexual problems were an essential ingredient in maintaining her overeating. It would probably have been impossible to change her eating habits successfully without first attending to their joint sexual difficulties with Mr. Osborn's full cooperation. In other cases, family members or friends might be utilized to provide cues for new behaviors or to provide reinforcers. Thus, we will see that a useful way to get Mrs. Smith to begin going out alone was for members of her family to deliberately provide cues for doing so (reminding her when it was time to do so, or arranging to meet her at a store) and to reinforce her with praise and affection after she had done so. Another common function of such "change agents" is to provide a model for new behaviors that the patient has not yet learned, but could acquire by watching and imitating. Models are also useful in demonstrating to the patient that a feared behavior does not in fact lead to aversive consequences when performed by the model.

A fourth important patient resource is the availability of reinforcers in general. Because the development of new behaviors so often depends on the use of reinforcers to increase their frequency and to maintain them, it is a great advantage if the patient's life contains pleasant events that can be used in this manner. An important source of reinforcement comes from family members and close friends, who can be asked to provide attention, affection, and verbal approval for desired new behaviors. Beside these social reinforcers, other types of reinforcement can be utilized, such as food, listening to music, reading, listening to TV, purchasing new clothing, or going to a movie. If the patient does not have a sufficient number of reinforcers available in his life, the therapist will usually help him to "build them in." In other words, he will help the patient arrange his activities and his environment so that pleasant events occur more frequently.

One further resource that often benefits the patient is the ability to form vivid imagery. As we discuss more fully later in the chapter, it is often possible to make significant behavior changes by having the patient engage in the new behaviors in imagery; that is, by imagining them very vividly under special conditions. Not all persons have the ability to learn to use their imagination as vividly as is needed for this process. For those who do, it represents one more set of behavioral techniques that permits the therapist increased flexibility in deciding which behavior change strategies to employ.

The skills and resources of the therapist also play a most important part in the success of therapy. In addition to clinical experience and technical knowledge, desirable qualities include organizational ability, patience, persistence, and a high activity level. Perhaps most important, a certain attitudinal quality is required of the therapist. A person who believes that he has no right to exercise direct influence over the patient, but that the patient must make his own decision at his own pace in order for proper growth to take place, would be very uncomfortable as a behavior therapist. In fact, any person whose beliefs about therapeutic progress include a nondirective attitude toward the patient would find it difficult to be successful as a behavior therapist.

## Designing the Treatment Strategy

As we have seen, there are usually a number of different ways to bring about the changes desired by a patient. Of course, the available ways are limited by the patient's resources and also by the range of technical skills possessed by the therapist. Within these constraints, the therapist selects the procedure that seems to offer the most economical way of reaching the patient's goal. More often than not, he modifies the strategy as more information is collected about the patient's difficulties.

How does the therapist know what will be the most economical procedure? Obviously, there is no way to be certain. A good rule of thumb is to try the simplest procedure first if there is no obvious reason why it should be unsuitable. A question that is often troublesome for the beginning behavior therapist is to determine the extent to which a patient's problem behavior is currently being actively maintained by events that would compete with and swamp the patient's efforts to learn new behaviors. For example, Mrs. Osborn's marital problems were systematically defeating her attempts to lose weight and, indeed, played a large part in causing her eating problem in the first place. Thus, it was necessary to recognize and work on these conflicts before new eating behaviors could be learned.

Not all problems are generated and maintained by events in the patient's environment, however. For example, although Mrs. Smith had not been able to go out alone for several years, we shall see that it was possible to initiate this new behavior simply by arranging for it to occur and by reinforcing it suitably. In her case, the events that had been preventing it were long-standing fearful thoughts that were *not* being actively reinforced at the present time and they were rather easily eliminated once Mrs. Smith became fully aware of them.

A number of extreme cases have been reported in the professional literature in which severe phobias of more than 20 years' standing have been eliminated by simple desensitization procedures. It is interesting to behavior therapy researchers that some problem behaviors persist for year after year even though they have little relevance in the person's current functioning, while other problem behaviors that may superficially appear very similar are being actively maintained by important day-to-day events in the patient's life. The former, such as Mrs. Smith's, are easily eliminated; the latter, such as Mrs. Osborn's, require much preliminary work. As we have said above, the behavior therapist usually tends to assume that the problem can be easily eliminated until he has good evidence to the contrary.

In summary, then, the behavior therapist looks for events that are actively preventing the patient from engaging in the desired behaviors. If none are apparent, the therapist implements a program to deliberately initiate and reinforce the desired behaviors. On the other hand, if there are events that are hindering or interfering with new learning, the therapist attempts to have the patient deal with and remove these events first. Sometimes these interfering events are present but do not become apparent until the patient suddenly runs into difficulties in trying to learn the desired behaviors.

In general, the behavior therapist will teach the patient the new, desired behaviors before helping him eliminate the old, unadaptive ones. There is a simple logic to this procedure: if unadaptive behaviors are eliminated and the patient is then faced with the same old problem situation, he is likely to do something else unadaptive unless he has specifically learned and practiced a new, adaptive behavior. This type of outcome is traditionally known as "symptom substitution," and is particularly important in cases where a patient consistently avoids an adaptive behavior because it is associated with anxiety or some other aversive consequence. Without the therapist's help in overcoming the anxiety as a first step, the patient would never be able to begin learning the adaptive behavior.

An example well known to behavior therapists is the history of the behavioral treatment of alcoholism. The use of nausea-inducing drugs such as antabuse was initiated in the 1940's and had a certain limited success. In this procedure, the patient would become acutely nauseated shortly after swallowing alcohol, and thus would be systematically punished for every instance of drinking. More recent behavioral approaches to the treatment of alcoholism have emphasized the need to initially assist the patient in resolving the conflicts which led to his misuse of alcohol in the first place. This is usually done in active collaboration with his family, and the patient is helped to learn new and more adaptive ways of handling these conflicts. After these steps have been accomplished, the excessive use of alcohol can be actively punished. Such programs have had a much higher success rate in treating alcoholism than programs which rely only on a punishment procedure.

A rather similar model is used in the treatment of deviant sexual behaviors. Persons who engage in exhibitionism or child molesting, for example, generally have difficulties in normal sexual expression. Thus, the therapist would first attend to the development of normal adult sexual behaviors. This often involves the reduction of anxiety associated with normal sexual expression, followed by the learning of needed sexual knowledge and the development of social skills and opportunities for social and sexual interaction. To repeat what was said above, factors are often present that are actively maintaining the problem behaviors and thus preventing therapeutic progress but are initially not apparent to either the patient or the therapist.

As a rule of thumb, if the patient stops making progress in a new learning situation, the therapist should start looking for events that are interfering with this learning. To repeat, clues about such interfering events may have been totally unavailable at the beginning of treatment but are often quite readily indentified at a later time. In other words, the therapist initially has little choice but to work on what is apparent to him and often has no way of predicting whether his strategy will need to be changed at a later time. Let us refer in advance to the case of Mrs. Fisher, described in Chapter 3. As will be seen, the therapist's initial attempt to remove her obsessional and fearful thoughts by using the simple cognitive procedure of thought-stopping produced no lasting gain. The therapist therefore began trying to identify reinforcers that might be maintaining Mrs. Fisher's distressing thoughts. The therapist was wrong on the first attempt to identify these reinforcers, but was correct on the second.

## Promoting Effective Learning

In the last twenty years or so, behavioral scientists have discovered a number of principles for bringing about rapid and effective learning. Many of these principles have now been in active use for some years in the armed forces, in business and industry, and in the school classroom. They are also actively employed by behavior therapists to increase the efficiency with which patients learn new, desired behaviors. We have already introduced some of these principles; let us now examine them more systematically.

First, the knowledge or behavior to be learned should be arranged in *small structured steps*. Attention should be given only to the next step in the sequence, which should always be sufficiently small so that the patient is almost certain to perform it correctly. Failure to master a step within a short space of time usually means that the step was too big, and the therapist should break it down into two or more smaller steps. There are several obvious advantages to a stepwise procedure. First, the patient has virtually no failure experiences; he is successful at practically every step. Second, he develops a sense of continuous progress, which is enhanced by continuous information feedback (see below). Third, each step requires only a relatively small amount of practice, so that new steps appear soon and the patient's motivation can be maintained. A common error made by beginning behavior therapists is to employ too few steps in a learning sequence, leading to frustration and declining interest on the patient's part.

A second principle is the importance of accurate *rehearsal* and repetitive *practice*. We cannot overemphasize the need to have the patient repeat the behavior over and over again until he gets it right. Usually, the behavior therapist first rehearses the behavior to be learned (or the particular step in the sequence) with the patient until he knows what is required of him. Homework assignments are then set involving sufficient repetitive practice for the patient to achieve the degree of mastery that the therapist considers necessary.

A third basic principle is the importance of *immediate feedback* of information about the patient's performance, whenever possible. There is absolutely no point in having the patient practice the wrong behavior, and learning will be most efficient if feedback is given immediately on the extent to which the patient's performance was accurate. Eventually, the patient will learn to observe himself and provide his own feedback on the adequacy of his behavior. In the beginning, however, it is highly important for the therapist to provide this information, coupled with a generous amount of support and encouragement. In this light, the importance of having "behavior change agents" available in the patient's environment to provide immediate feedback can be better appreciated.

Our discussion of immediate feedback and encouragement brings us close to a formal procedure for developing new behaviors called *shaping*. Shaping refers to the provision of immediate reinforcement for successive approximations to the desired behavior until eventually the behavior itself is performed. Another term used by behavior therapists is a *hierarchy*, referring to a graded series of steps involving the same general behavior. A hierarchy begins with a step that is easily manageable by the patient and ends with behaviors that are desired but currently well beyond the patient's capacity. In Chapter 3 we describe the use of hierarchies of situations for teaching Mrs. Fisher to become more assertive, to express anger more appropriately, to accept anger more comfortably, to tolerate feared objects, and to engage in normal social behavior.

A fourth basic principle in rapid and effective learning is the importance of setting highly *explicit goals*. According to the old saying, if you don't know where you're going, you won't know when you get there. In modern classroom instruction, for example, the formulation of goals for learning has reached a high level of sophistication and often involves specific criterion behaviors. An example of a criterion in arithmetic for fourth graders would be to achieve a certain minimum score on each of a series of exercises which test for specific operational skills. Another example is found in the driving tests that are given by many state Departments of Motor Vehicles. Here, each person is required to successfully demonstrate a number of specific driving skills with no more than a specified maximum number of errors.

The question of whether explicit goals can be set for the treatment of human psychological difficulties has been studied by researchers in behavior therapy, and they have shown that explicit goal setting is indeed effective here also. As a matter of fact, certain kinds of human difficulties are best handled by what is perhaps the most extreme form of structured goal setting: the formal contract. For example, behavioral contracting, both formal and informal, is a necessity in working with acting-out adolescents. The written behavioral contract specifies what behaviors the client agrees to perform, and what consequences will follow if the client does perform the behaviors and also if he does not perform them. The behavior therapist generally does not adopt such extremes with most patients, but does negotiate an explicit agreement with the patient concerning goals. This negotiation includes a discussion as to what final goals seem most realistic, alternative means of accomplishing these goals, an agreement as to the most desirable course of action, and the patient's acceptance of the likely outcome.

## Procedures for New Learning

So far we have glossed over the actual procedures that the therapist uses for teaching the patient new behaviors and for unlearning old behaviors. We have referred frequently to the need for increasing or decreasing the frequency of a particular behavior (or for eliminating it altogether), but we have not yet described how this is done. We now attend in detail to this question.

There is no perfect way to classify methods of learning. The four categories used below are not mutually exclusive, but they offer a convenient way to understand this rather complex area. These categories are: (a) *reinforcement and punishment* procedures; (b) *cognitive* procedures; (c) *modeling* procedures; and (d) *imagery* procedures. The last of these categories, imagery procedures, is not really a separate category at all, but is an interesting and flexible method of applying the other three sets of procedures.

### Reinforcement and Punishment Procedures

The frequency of a behavior can be changed by altering its consequences, and such changes involve the use of reinforcement or punishment. Formal discussion of the principles of reinforcement are beyond the scope of this book. Let us introduce some of the major concepts and illustrate their use. The term "reinforcement" is used to describe procedures which result in an increase in behavior, while "punishment" refers to procedures which result in a decrease in behavior.

*Positive reinforcement* is familiar to most people as a way of increasing desired behaviors by adding a desired consequence. A women who succeeds in increasing the frequency of her partner's sexual advances by systematically responding positively to every advance is using positive reinforcement. Of course, it is possible to unwittingly reinforce behavior that you would rather not have. As we will see below, Mrs. Smith's husband unwittingly reinforced her depressive behavior by being especially attentive and affectionate at those times.

Reinforcement can also involve the removal of something unpleasant, since behaviors tend to increase in frequency if they are followed by the removal of an unpleasant event. The mother who attends to her child only when he is whining incessantly is likely to increase his frequency of whining by positively reinforcing it with attention. If her attention does result in a temporary decrease in whining, and she therefore attends to his whining more often in the future, it would be said that her attending behavior had been negatively reinforced.

*Punishment* is just what it appears to be—a procedure resulting in a decrease in behavior, usually through an unpleasant consequence. If the woman in our former example sought to decrease her partner's sexual advances by calling him "disgusting" or "a bungler," and as a result he stopped making advances, we would say that his behavior had been decreased through punishment.

If a behavior is followed by no consequences at all, it is likely to decrease in frequency and eventually all but disappear. This procedure for decreasing a behavior is called *extinction*. If the woman had completely ignored her partner's sexual requests and they had disappeared for that reason, we would say that extinction had taken place.

We have already introduced the next concept, *shaping*. In a shaping procedure, reinforcement is given for any behavior that is in any way close to the desired behavior. Once these "approximate" behaviors are being performed at a high enough rate, reinforcement is given only for those behaviors that are closest to the desired behavior. Thus, shaping is a continuous process in which reinforcement is given for successively closer approximations to the desired behavior. A simple example of shaping can be seen in the college student who established the goal of spending two hours studying each evening. The reinforcement he selected was TV watching, and he made a behavioral contract with himself to watch TV only if he had completed his minimum study assignment for the evening.

Initially, his assignment was to study for at least fifteen minutes per evening, after which TV watching was available. When he was successfully meeting this minimum requirement four week nights out of five, he moved the task one step closer to his final goal by setting himself a minimum study time of half an hour per evening before TV watching was permitted. The next approximation in his plan involved 45 minutes of studying, then one hour, and he proceeded with further fifteen minute increments until his goal of two hours was reached.

Another important learning procedure involving reinforcement is *discrimination training*. Here, the goal is to perform a particular behavior in certain specific situations but not others. The first step is to make sure that the two kinds of situations can be clearly recognized as different; that is, to ensure that each has its own distinctive cues. Then the person is systematically reinforced for performing the behavior in the appropriate situation, while no reinforcement is provided for performing the behavior in the inappropriate situation. Verbal or cognitive cues ("That's right;" "That's not right") play an important part in discrimination learning. Adaptive social behavior requires the learning of many discriminations, such as when the expresssion of anger is appropriate and when it is not, or when a sexual advance will be reinforced and when it will not. Behavior therapists commonly help their patients arrange situations in which such discriminations can be successfully learned.

## Cognitive Learning Procedures

Behavior therapists have recently recognized the importance of cognitions or thoughts and self-instructions in cueing and maintaining behavior. These procedures are by no means new; in fact, traditional "home remedies" for common psychological problems have often involved the use of cognitive procedures. Thus, many years ago Emile Coué recommended that personal difficulties could be successfully resolved by daily repetition of the thought "Every day, in every way, I'm getting better and better." Norman Vincent Peale's highly influential book *The Power of Positive Thinking* has also advocated the benefits of increasing the frequency of adaptive thoughts.

The simplest use of cognitive procedures in learning involves written or spoken instructions. Much of our everyday behavior is cued by instruction, either from the environment or from within ourselves. Formal classroom learning has always relied heavily on spoken and written verbal instruction to promote learning. Educational and behavioral researchers nowadays are making rapid advances in determining the kinds of learning tasks for which cognitive learning procedures are in fact the best, and under what circumstances other learning procedures are better employed. It has been an important discovery in the treatment of autistic children, for example, that the most effective initial learning can be achieved not through cognitive learning but through reinforcement learning. On the other hand, some interesting recent research with impulsive children suggests that such children respond well to systematic instruction designed to increase their use of cognitive processes.

Today, Coué's procedure might be termed *cognitive rehearsal*. A behavior therapist employing it would probably seek to increase its effectiveness by having the patient systematically follow each set of positive self-statements with a pleasant event. That is, he would arrange for the new adaptive thought to be systematically reinforced. The therapist would probably also have the patient employ specific statements focused on a particular area in which the patient's beliefs about himself were not in line with reality.

Let us briefly illustrate the therapeutic use of cognitive procedures with reference to Mrs. Gordon, a patient who was timid, unassertive, and had great difficulty in meeting new people. The therapist's initial assessment procedures showed that an important factor maintaining these timid behaviors was that Mrs. Gordon continually thought a series of pessimistic, negative thoughts about herself. The therapist set out to deliberately replace these negative, unadaptive thoughts with positive thoughts which the patient also believed but actually engaged in at a low frequency. Thus, she was asked to write at least 20 times a day: "I am an intelligent, worthwhile person and people will be interested in what I have to say." She was to do this immediately before drinking a cup of coffee (assuming she was alone at the time), so that the coffee would serve as a reinforcer. This procedure increased the frequency with which Mrs. Gordon made new, positive self-statements, and thus increased the likelihood that she would recall such self-statements at times when she normally made negative statements about herself.

The broad and general area of helping patients to recognize unadaptive and self-defeating statements and to systematically replace them with adaptive self-statements has been termed *cognitive restructuring*. Psychologist Albert Ellis' well-known rational-emotive psychotherapy involves these procedures as one of its most basic aspects. Paying attention to self-verbalizations helps patients to recognize the thoughts that serve as cues for problem behaviors. Most commonly, patients are involved in a complex sequence or chain of behaviors involving external cues, thoughts, and feelings. For example, Mrs. Gordon's father-in-law would often state something with which she disagreed (an external cue). Mrs. Gordon would then think to herself: "I don't agree with that. I should tell him what I think" (a thought). She would then experience an increase in anxiety (a feeling), and would handle this by thinking: "My opinion isn't worth much, and he probably wouldn't be interested in it anyway" (another thought). At this point, Mrs. Gordon's anxiety would decrease markedly and she would feel more comfortable. This sequence illustrates how her negative self-statements were continually reinforced by a reduction in anxiety. In this way, Mrs. Gordon's negative self-statements caused her to consistently avoid a situation with which she was having difficulty. In therapy, cognitive rehearsal was used in combination with other procedures to enable Mrs. Gordon to comfortably express her own opinion to her father-in-law.

A number of years ago, psychiatrist Joseph Wolpe developed an interesting cognitive learning procedure for reducing persistent obsessional thoughts. Called *thought stopping*, this procedure relies initially on the distraction effect of an unexpected noise to terminate the obsessional thought. The patient is asked to get the thought firmly in mind; then the therapist startles him by loudly saying "Stop!" The patient is asked to acknowledge that the thought did indeed disappear, and the sequence is then repeated a number of times. As a next step, the patient himself is taught to exclaim "Stop!" at the appropriate time. Finally, the patient is taught to yell "Stop!" to himself in imagery (see section on imaginal learning). If successful, the patient will have learned a specific self-control technique for removing the thought when it occurs. Some therapists who employ this technique also teach the patient to think a pleasant thought immediately after saying "Stop!" or a thought which is contradictory to the obsessional thought.

Many readers will have recognized that some aspects of cognitive learning procedures as employed in behavior therapy bear a similarity to procedures that have come to be known as "brainwashing" or "mind control." It should be noted that the accepted procedures of religious observance (individual and corporate prayer, hymn singing, Bible reading, and other ritualistic aspects of worship) also share many aspects in common with both cognitive behavior therapy procedures and mind control. Indeed, most of the institutions (family, school, etc.) which help raise children as civilized, social people attuned to a particular cultural environment employ such procedures.

In behavior therapy, the use of these cognitive learning procedures is deliberately overt. Therapists carefully explain what they are doing in order that their patients will be able to use the procedures as tools in other life situations. Such openness tends to highlight their advantages, but also makes it clear how they might be abused. Thus, in evaluating the ethics of using cognitive learning procedures, the focus should be on evaluating the purpose to which they are put and ensuring that the patient is fully aware and deliberately chooses to participate in their use. In the therapeutic use of cognitive procedures, the therapist and patient should always agree fully on what thoughts are to be changed and on the overall goals, which are to help the patient regain his own control over thoughts which are currently not in his control and are thereby causing difficulties for him.

## Learning through Modeling

Learning through modeling is also a fairly recent addition to the knowledge and technology of the behavior therapist. The development of this field of knowledge is due in large measure to the work of psychologist Albert Bandura. Modeling is a scientific term for what is more commonly called learning by imitation, learning by example, or observational learning. The essential aspect of modeling is observing a person, real or implied, who models or demonstrates the behavior to be learned. By "implied" we mean that the model might be represented in words or pictures dealing with the behavior, or might be an imaginal representation.

It is now known that many social behaviors, perhaps the majority of them, are learned initially by children and adolescents through modeling, and are maintained by reinforcement (or extinguished for the lack of it). Thus, perhaps the most common reason why a person might lack social skills with the opposite sex is the failure to be exposed to appropriate models during the adolescent years when these skills are normally learned and/or the lack of opportunities for reinforced practice of these skills. In attempting to remedy such problems, the behavior therapist would arrange for the patient to be systematically exposed to situations in which the required behaviors are being modeled, followed by systematic rehearsal through a hierarchy of situations ranging from preliminary to complex. Some behavior therapists believe that this type of combined learning package, which they term "participant modeling," is the most effective of all procedures that are currently in use for helping patients overcome problems involving both strong fears and strong avoidance behaviors.

In selecting an appropriate model for behaviors that need to be learned by a particular patient, the therapist pays careful attention to certain needed characteristics of the model. The influence of a model on another person's behavior is most powerful under the following four conditions: (a) if the model is a high prestige figure; (b) if the model's own behavior is seen to be reinforced; (c) if the model is similar to the patient in age, sex, and other obvious characteristics; and (d) if the model is perceived as warm, nurturant, and competent.

### Imaginal Procedures

The discovery by behavior therapists that many new behaviors can be successfully learned by imagining them rather than by doing or seeing them in real life has been an important contribution to the technology of behavior therapy. The use of imagery in the treatment of psychological disorders is by no means new, since hypnosis is based on the use of imagery. One of the drawbacks of hypnosis, however, has always been its mysterious nature and its association with the entertainment industry. An essential characteristic of imagery procedures in behavior therapy is that, unlike hypnosis, the entire sequence of events is kept completely within the control of the patient, who regulates the nature of the images and their intensity. We have already discussed in Chapter 1 the fact that thoughts are known to follow many of the same principles of learning as overt behaviors. Thus it should come as no surprise to find that new learning can be brought about by working with images, or "illustrated thoughts."

What does the behavior therapist mean by the use of imagery? Basically, it is meant that the patient engages in a very vivid and realistic "daydream" of the behavior or situation of interest. The ability to develop vivid imagery is a skill that must usually be learned, and most people can master it in a few hours. The degree of vividness required in images for effective behavior therapy is more than simply seeing a mental picture of oneself in the situation. The critical aspect is that the patient must, from his subjective viewpoint, actually *be* there. To get the flavor of what we mean by imagery, think of a time when you were in a boring situation (class, lecture, or meeting, etc.) and you escaped by daydreaming. Suddenly you were in some other place, perhaps a very pleasant situation, perhaps one you were looking forward to. Or perhaps you were finishing up an argument with your spouse or rehearsing how to stand up to your boss. The important point is that although physically you were still in the classroom, mentally you were experiencing another situation as realistically as if you were actually there. We are usually brought sharply back to reality from such mental trips by a strong stimulus, such as a loud noise, someone's voice, or physical movement. Regular night dreaming is another example of the experience of imagery. In fact, one popular theory of dreaming is that it is a natural process of working through one's conflicts and difficulties through imagery.

Many things that can be learned through overt behavior can also be learned in imagery, at least for their initial stages. A well-known example involves learning to reduce anxiety about a specific feared situation or object, such as fear of public speaking. Here the therapist and patient together develop a hierarchy of situations involving public speaking, ranging from mildly fear arousing (such as watching a speaker on TV) to intensely fear arousing (such as waiting one's turn to speak before a large audience). The patient systematically imagines the first situation for a series of short intervals until he no longer experiences it as fear arousing. Then he moves to the next image and repeats the process. This procedure, developed by psychiatrist Joseph Wolpe, is known as *systematic desensitization*, and is often carried out while the patient is in a state of deep muscle relaxation. It was originally believed that complete muscle relaxation was an essential part of the procedure, but most behavior therapists now believe that the relaxation is unnecessary. However, it often has a helpful effect, probably through aiding concentration by keeping out external distractions and by magnifying the patient's awareness of internal thoughts and feelings. A case example employing imaginal desensitization to alleviate a longstanding phobia of rain and storms is described in Chapter 4.

Systematic desensitization can also be carried out using a hierarchy of real-life situations rather than imagery, and at times working in real life is the preferred procedure. However, the use of imagery is sometimes preferable for a number of reasons. For example, an imagery procedure can be conducted entirely in the therapist's office, and the imaginal situations can be created and dismissed almost instantaneously, once the patient is fully trained to do so. Also, the therapist can add additional steps in the hierarchy at short notice if the patient appears to need them. Indeed, for some phobic problems, such as fear of flying or fear of being alone, it is difficult or impossible to create the situations effectively in real life in the early stages of treatment.

Imagery procedures can also be utilized for teaching patients new adaptive behaviors, such as assertiveness and social skills. Here, the patient engages in a graded series of vivid images involving being in an interpersonal situation and making the appropriate response. The imaginal characters in the images would respond in a variety of different ways, ranging from highly accepting to highly rejecting. Then the patient would in turn practice a variety of ways of handling these responses. Generally, the overall content that is to be utilized in such an image would be developed in detail by the therapist and patient together.

Modeling procedures can also be used in imagery. Here, the patient would engage in an image in which a model performs the desired behavior and is reinforced for it. Or in the case of an overweight patient, for example, the image might involve an overweight model eating taboo food and suffering highly aversive consequences.

Another way in which imagery can be helpful in the course of behavior therapy is in helping the patient to identify thoughts and feelings associated with a situation which he habitually avoids, perhaps to such an extent that he has no clear idea of the thoughts and feelings that are associated with it. Knowledge of such thoughts and feelings is often extremely important for assessment and for treatment planning, for the thoughts and feelings might be the key events that are cueing and maintaining the patient's difficulties. When imagery procedures are used for bringing about new learning, this kind of new information about as yet unrecognized thoughts and feelings often becomes available to the patient, perhaps analogous to "insight" during verbal psychotherapy.

The two essential factors in teaching successful imagery are (a) freedom from external stimulation; and (b) a large variety of details. External stimulation is minimized by using a quiet room and having the patient close his eyes and relax his muscles. In order to develop an image that is as detailed as possible, the patient and therapist first agree on the most important aspects of the image; for example, being in a room full of people. The patient is asked to make the image "come to life" by specifying the actual place where it occurs, the other people who are present, and a systematic account of all other possible details that the image will contain. Having prepared the details of the image in this manner, the therapist then asks the patient to close his eyes and "be" in the situation. Initially, the therapist might list the details one by one, and the patient adds them to his image. The patient might also add any further details that would make the image even more vivid. The therapist often arranges for the patient to give a signal (perhaps by moving a finger or opening his eyes) if the image becomes too anxiety arousing or disturbing in some other way. Sometimes the therapist and patient will have agreed in advance that the patient will "stick it out" through a high-anxiety experience, as one method of teaching the patient to cope with new situations. The question of when to use such "flooding" procedures is complex and requires skill and experience on the therapist's part.

## The Need for Self-Management

In our rather brief description of learning procedures we made no specific reference to one very important practical aspect of learning in behavior therapy, namely, self-management. A patient cannot be regarded as successfully treated until he has learned the skills that will enable him to continue performing the new adaptive behaviors that the behavior therapist has taught him. For patients in verbal psychotherapy, this matter has often been left more or less to chance. In behavior therapy, however, the matter of teaching the patient to maintain his changes after the end of therapy is regarded as an integral part of the therapy procedure. The topic of self-management or self-control is an interesting and relatively new one, and is analyzed in detail in Chapter 7.

## Application to Case Examples

In Chapter 1 we introduced three case illustrations: Mrs. Osborn, with an obesity problem; Mrs. Smith, with an overdependency problem; and Mr. Watts, whose life had lost its meaning. We now proceed with the application of behavior therapy treatment principles to each of these persons in turn. You may wish to refresh your memory on the case history material presented earlier and the behavioral assessment and analysis for each case.

### Mrs. Osborn

The reader will recall that Mrs. Osborn surrounded herself with attractive snacking food but did not eat regular breakfast or lunch. Also, her husband constantly criticized her and completely overlooked most of her positive behavior, such as her conscientiousness. A routine discussion of their sexual history had shown that the husband had often had difficulty keeping an erection, and that he tended to blame it on the fact that his wife was overweight and thus not physically attractive. The more he criticized her, the less acceptable she felt, and the more she would avoid him and gain her satisfactions in eating.

In order to help this couple to increase the frequency of positive sexual responses toward each other, the therapist introduced them to some "sensate focusing" exercises that were developed for this purpose by Masters and Johnson. Under the "no demand" conditions created by these exercises, Mr. Osborn found that he could consistently achieve and maintain his erection. Working with the Osborns on their sexual adjustment was a complex task that occupied a considerable amount of time throughout treatment. However, they made steady progress as a couple. Treatment of sexual problems such as this one is discussed in detail in Chapter 6.

The therapist also worked to reduce the frequency of negative statements which Mr. Osborn made about his wife, and to increase his frequency of positive statements. Negative statements were reduced by having Mr. Osborn keep a written record of them as identified by Mrs. Osborn. For each critical statement, he was required to make a positive statement that was true about her from a list that the Osborns prepared with the therapist's help.

Mrs. Osborn was next instructed to make a number of basic changes in her food-related behavior. She was a given a list of techniques to reduce the number of food cues in her environment, such as keeping all food out of sight, cooking just enough food for a meal so that there would be no leftovers, and keeping tempting foods in places that were difficult to get at. She was also helped to structure all necessary food-related behavior, such as shopping after eating rather than when she was hungry, and buying only what was on her carefully prepared shopping list. After two weeks of practice at these tasks and careful record keeping of what she actually ate, she agreed to maintain a balanced diet of 1200 calories. She was instructed to eat breakfast and lunch regularly and thus to reduce the probability of impulsive snacking in the afternoon by not being so hungry. Also, the therapist helped her plan alternate activities away from food cues during the afternoon, and helped her develop a list of low-calorie snacking food, such as raw carrots, that could be systematically included in her schedule. Most of these changes would be termed "stimulus-control" procedures.

Once Mrs. Osborn's husband saw that she was serious about losing weight, he was more than willing to help her structure her daily activities in order to provide positive satisfactions for her and to help her avoid eating. Other new behaviors included her plans to buy desirable clothes that were slightly smaller than the ones she currently wore, to serve as reinforcers for losing weight, and the development of a regular exercise program maintained by social approval from her husband. Throughout the period she was instructed to weigh herself upon arising each morning and to plot her weight on a chart kept in full view in the bathroom.

Mrs. Osborn lost an average of one and half pounds per week over nine months, with some fluctuations at critical points in therapy. One such point was, for example, during a two-week period of intense conflict with her husband. The therapist saw them together and was able to persuade Mr. Osborn to articulate his strong fears that she would leave him because he feared he could not satisfy her sexually. Mrs. Osborn successfully lost her 60 pounds and has maintained this loss for a two-year period within the new context of improved interpersonal and sexual relationships with her husband.

## Mrs. Smith

The reader will recall that Mrs. Smith became extremely anxious when alone, and that these fears had appeared within the last five years. Shortly before they began, one of the Smiths' children had left home and another planned to do so shortly.

In trying to identify cues associated with Mrs. Smith's going out by herself and cues about the terrible things that she feared would happen to her when alone, the therapist reviewed her adolescence and early adulthood. Mrs. Smith was unable to recall such fears occurring at any other time in her life, but she was able to report that she had never been left alone in the house as an adolescent, nor was she permitted to go out by herself because "nice girls don't go out alone." She was married at age 20 after working for one year as a salesperson, very much against her parents' will. Nevertheless, she had greatly enjoyed this brief period of work outside the house.

It began to appear that her fear of being at home alone had developed only in the last few months and that her more basic fear was of going out alone. Because there did not seem to be any obvious events that were actively maintaining her fear of going out alone, the therapist decided to make an attempt to increase this behavior directly by positive reinforcement. He enlisted family members as change agents, and in consultation with the family and Mrs. Smith constructed a hierarchy of structured steps involving going out of the house. The hierarchy included, for example, being met by her husband at a store two blocks from the house, and going out to mail a letter. Once the therapist convinced her that this procedure was by far the quickest way to solve her problem, she agreed to try. Mrs. Smith made good progress on the hierarchy for three weeks, but then found it impossible to do any further assignments.

In order to search for cues that might be triggering excessive fear at this point, the therapist trained Mrs. Smith in imagery and had her rehearse the next three assignments as imaginal events. Mrs. Smith experienced the greatest amount of anxiety while imagining going to a department store and spending some leisure time there.

The therapist's questioning revealed that her thoughts during this event had centered on the possibility of getting a job at the store, and her vivid recollection of how intensely her parents had been opposed to her working as a salesperson. The therapist requested other family members to attend the next session and opened the topic of Mrs. Smith's getting a job. All were surprised but very enthusiastic and began discussing how to reorganize the household schedule and chores. Mrs. Smith's husband voiced some initial reluctance but soon recognized this hesitation as his own problem. Mrs. Smith now works three days a week in a local store and spends a considerable amount of time discussing with her husband the adjustments that they must make as their children leave home.

## Mr. Watts

In selecting strategies for working with Mr. Watts, several factors were immediately apparent to the therapist. First, the aversiveness of many aspects of his work and home life had tended to make him perceive all aspects of life as aversive. Second, in order to stop him from withdrawing from his environment entirely, he would need extensive opportunities to experience positive thoughts and feelings.

The therapist asked Mr. Watts to make a list of things that he enjoyed doing. Mr. Watts was not able to come up with even a single item. The therapist then asked him to make a list of things he used to like doing. This time he was able to prepare a small list of items, such as caring for the lawn (the family currently hired a professional service to do this work), reading the paper from beginning to end, attending the local high school football games, and eating lunch with his colleagues at work and joking with them. However, he was simply unwilling to consider initiating any of these activities again.

The therapist therefore focused on the task of removing some of the aversive events from Mr. Watts' environment. Together they rehearsed conversations with two of Mr. Watts' children, in which he explained to them that they would have to earn a substantial amount of their own college costs. In their rehearsal, the therapist had Mr. Watts practice what he feared he would have to do, namely, defend himself against angry and disappointed children. However, when Mr. Watts held the conversation in real life, he was surprised to find that his children readily agreed, saying that they had fully expected to pay most of their own costs. Thus reinforced for asserting himself, Mr. Watts was more easily persuaded by the therapist to tackle further tasks involving family demands for money. Another group of situations which required much more rehearsal and reassurance by the therapist involved Mr. Watts telling his subordinates at work that they would henceforth be expected to deal with most of their complaints themselves, and to consult him only on policy matters.

At this point in therapy, Mr. Watts requested to return to the challenge of deliberately building pleasant events into his life. As a first step, he negotiated with his wife an agreement that they would engage in some social activities that were specifically satisfying to each of them. During these weeks, Mr. Watts found himself becoming easily angry at people and at times even losing his temper, something he had not done since he was a child. The therapist asked him to keep notes on such situations, and together they attempted to pinpoint the kinds of situations that would indeed warrant the direct expression of anger, and the kinds that would not. Mr. Watts' feelings of meaninglessness had entirely disappeared by this time, but he requested to work with the therapist for an extended period on a number of the specific dissatisfactions that they had identified.

## Concluding Comment

The reader will doubtless have many questions about these cases. For example, why did the therapist not follow up more directly on the possibility that Mrs. Smith's difficulties were caused mainly by the departure of her children from the home? Or why did the therapist not try a thought-stopping procedure to help Mr. Watts with his thoughts of meaninglessness? The reader should understand that with any specific case, certain decisions are made by the therapist on the basis of experience and to some extent on the basis of trial and error. In the interest of brevity of reporting, much of this material has been omitted from these three case reports. In the next chapter, we present a single case in detail from start to finish, taking the reader step by step through the stages of behavioral assessment and treatment as they actually occurred. We have tried to present sufficient detail to capture the flavor of the problem and of the therapeutic work as it actually developed.

# 3

# Behavior Therapy Applied: The Case of Mrs. Fisher

In Chapter 1 we introduced a number of basic aspects of behavior therapy: its history, its status within the field of therapeutic endeavors, its philosophical basis, and its scientific underpinnings in behavioral science. We also introduced the way in which behavior therapists relate to their patients. Next, we introduced three real-life human problems, and discussed how to define them in a manner suitable for behavior therapy and how to assess them in order to understand the ways in which they are cued and maintained. In Chapter 2 we continued this basic overview of behavior therapy, introducing the way in which the patient's resources are assessed, and describing the major technical procedures for bringing about new learning. Also discussed were the ways in which the therapist selects the particular techniques to apply in bringing about the desired changes, and the way in which these techniques were actually utilized in working with the three problem cases introduced in Chapter 1.

In the present chapter, these decisions, techniques, and procedures are further illustrated in a complete case description of a young married woman with multiple problems of rather serious nature. What follows is a factual account of this actual case, presented accurately except for minor changes which ensure the privacy of the patient and her family. The account is presented with permission of Mrs. Fisher and her husband.

In following this material, the reader should understand that the course of therapy did not proceed quite as "neatly" as the written account conveys. For example, certain aspects of Mrs. Fisher's problem which are not identified until later in the account were in fact discussed briefly at an earlier time. Also, some of the behavior change techniques are described as though they were carried out only over a week or two. In fact, most procedures were carried out over many weeks. Third, part of each therapy session was spent in reviewing all of Mrs. Fisher's learning and ensuring that she was carrying out her new procedures appropriately. The sole purpose in simplifying the written account is to make it manageable for the reader, and the essential character of the case has been maintained.

## Background Information

Mrs. Fisher, a 26-year-old married woman with a four-year-old son, Peter, was referred to one of the authors for treatment of her mushrooming obsessional fears that she would kill her child, and perhaps also other children. She also experienced persistent and overwhelming anxiety in her everyday life which she attributed to these obsessions. Mrs. Fisher was a graduate nurse but was not currently working. Her 27-year-old husband had completed two years of college and worked as an administrator in a small company. The Fishers had been married five years and lived in their own home. Mrs. Fisher specifically requested help in ridding herself of the obsessional fears and thoughts and also in reducing her general level of anxiety. As will be seen later, Mrs. Fisher's inability to express anger appropriately was identified as a third major problem area, and marital conflicts constituted a fourth. A fifth problem area, possibly related to her fear of killing children, was strong anxiety about death in her family.

These problems were identified as the result of an initial interview with Mrs. Fisher herself and a second interview with Mrs. Fisher and her husband together, plus the Minnesota Multiphasic Personality Inventory (MMPI) and a written biographical data sheet completed by each of them.

The history of Mrs. Fisher's difficulties was as follows. She first recognized the existence of a problem several years ago when she was ten weeks pregnant with her child. A friend who had visited her the previous day had called later to say that she might have rubella (German measles), a disease which Mrs. Fisher knew as a nurse could seriously endanger the fetus. Shortly after, while driving her car, Mrs. Fisher suddenly experienced a strong fear that she would run over a child that she saw. This experience frightened her very much, and it recurred 15 or 20 times during her pregnancy, along with the fear that her own child would be born deformed. Her general day-to-day anxiety also mounted considerably over this time.

Intensifying her fears about her own child was the fact that Mrs. Fisher had not had a prenatal blood test to find out whether she was immune to rubella. (If the blood test indicated that she was immune to rubella, then the child could not be deformed as a result of the exposure to it.) Mrs. Fisher now arranged for a blood test immediately, but unfortunately the laboratory lost her blood sample. By the time a second sample had been taken and analyzed, six weeks had passed, and each day Mrs. Fisher became more and more convinced that she had done something that would harm her baby through no intention of her own. She sought advice in handling these fearful thoughts from her obstetrician, who responded only with reassurance that the fears were simply due to her pregnancy and would disappear once the baby was born.

Mrs. Fisher gave birth to a normal baby boy. However, her fears increased in intensity, and she now found herself the victim of a new fear that she would poison the child. When the baby was seven months old, both her husband and the baby became ill at the same time. Mrs. Fisher promptly experienced a "nervous breakdown," for which she was placed in the psychiatric wing of a general hospital with a diagnosis of "postpartum depression." (It is not uncommon for mothers of newborn children to become quite depressed soon after the birth. Depression related to the birth in some manner is called postpartum depression. However, in Mrs. Fisher's case, the behavior therapist believed that the depression was caused by other factors and that this diagnosis was incorrect.) Mrs. Fisher was treated with a lengthy series of electroconvulsive shock treatments, followed by ten months of weekly psychotherapy sessions within a psychoanalytic orientation. Mrs. Fisher's specific fears of killing children and also her general anxiety diminished to a manageable level and were maintained there for about a year. She then began to feel impelled to lock up any household articles that she might use to kill her child, such as aspirin and other drugs, cleaning liquids, pins, needles, and ointments. All of these were gradually put under lock and key. Mrs. Fisher insisted that her husband keep the key, thus restricting considerably her household activities during the day.

When Peter was two and a half years old, he developed large hives of unknown origin all over his body the day after a routine visit to the pediatrician. Mrs. Fisher's obsessional fears immediately regained their old strength and she returned to continue her psychotherapy. Twelve months later, Mrs. Fisher's condition had steadily deteriorated, and at this point she was referred to the behavior therapist. At the time of the initial visit, Mrs. Fisher's difficulties included obsessional fears that she would kill her own child, other children, and pregnant women. Although her husband and mother were both initially quite alarmed by her phobias, they would now become impatient with her and tell her not to take herself so seriously. At these times Mrs. Fisher felt angry and misunderstood.

As a result of her difficulties, Mrs. Fisher's functioning was greatly restricted. For example, all social life was eliminated for both her and her husband. Also, she was unable to see friends and neighbors because of her fear of poisoning them or their children. This was particularly distressing because her neighbors valued her friendship and her nursing knowledge, and they would frequently seek her advice on medical questions related to their children or themselves. Further, she was unable to visit the pediatrician or obstetrician unless accompanied by another adult, because she feared she would tamper with the medication and thus harm a later patient. Exacerbating her difficulties were vaguely recognized fears that she or her child would be poisoned by other people. Another massive constraint on her functioning, as described above, was her need to have many household items locked up and under the control of her husband. Her many interpersonal difficulties included an intense fear of being criticized and a complete inability to express justifiable criticism, assertion, or anger appropriately. Finally, approximately once a week Mrs. Fisher would become uncontrollably and hysterically enraged at her husband and at these times she would threaten to commit suicide.

Mrs. Fisher's father, a steam fitter by trade, died of a stroke when she was eight years old. The subject of the father's death always remained a taboo subject among family members. Mrs. Fisher's mother remarried when she was 13 years old, and she was quite ambivalent in her feelings about her stepfather. Mrs. Fisher was the second of four siblings, all but one college educated. There was no significant history of psychological disorders in the family. Mrs. Fisher described her early childhood as happy and later childhood as less so.

## Initial Formulation

Mrs. Fisher was a slim, attractive woman who dressed casually but neatly. Although she was extremely tense during the initial interview, she related well and communicated clearly in spite of her high anxiety. She was a warm, likable person but timid and unassertive in manner. The MMPI profile supported the therapist's impression that Mrs. Fisher was best characterized as severely neurotic with some possible difficulties involving thought processes. It also reflected her chronic high anxiety and her tendency to engage in confused thinking and in obsessional thoughts about unusual or trivial matters. The test also indicated that she was quite a dependent person with a poor self-concept, and that she was likely to experience physical problems such as headaches or insomnia.

At this early stage in the assessment process, it was not clear what cues and reinforcers were maintaining Mrs. Fisher's obsessional fears. However, difficulties in expressing and receiving anger were much more clearly defined, and it seemed likely that these difficulties would interfere directly with the therapeutic work. Specifically, her inability to express and receive anger appropriately seemed to be a direct threat to the marital relationship and would also be likely to interfere with the therapeutic relationship if she were not able to express her annoyance or other negative feelings toward the therapist when she experienced them. The therapist also made a plausible guess that anger was a strong contributing factor, and perhaps even a direct cue, for Mrs. Fisher's obsessional thoughts. Thus, several purposes would be served by assisting Mrs. Fisher to recognize and express anger more appropriately, to receive anger more comfortably from others, and to be more appropriately assertive. In exploring situations in which Mrs. Fisher could have been more assertive, the therapist discovered that her perception of herself was quite out of line with reality, since she saw herself as a weak, unlikable person whose friendship was not valued by others. It also seemed important, therefore, to help her develop a more accurate and positive view of herself.

To summarize, it appeared to the therapist that Mrs. Fisher would have great difficulty in making any changes related to her present problems unless she had a more positive, realistic view of herself and was able to express and receive anger more appropriately. It was possible, but not certain, that her difficulties with anger were directly responsible for cueing and/or maintaining her fearful obsessions. Several courses of therapeutic action were therefore considered initially, and briefly discussed with Mrs. Fisher: improving her negative self-image; teaching skills for handling anger; and working directly on the fearful obsessions.

## Treatment Procedures

### Thought Stopping

After reviewing with a colleague these alternatives and Mrs. Fisher's reactions to them, the therapist decided that it would be most appropriate to first try a direct procedure for eliminating Mrs. Fisher's unwanted obsessional thoughts through a simple thought-stopping technique. Accordingly, the procedure was explained to Mrs. Fisher and she was asked to close her eyes and become fully involved in her obsessional fears about harming her son. After two or three seconds she signaled that she had done so by raising her finger. The therapist shouted "Stop!" and was successful in startling the thought away (Mrs. Fisher jumped and her eyes flew open). The therapist spent the next half hour taking her through the further steps of this procedure as described in Chapter 2, and then set the homework assignment of practicing for fifteen minutes per day. She was also to employ the procedure whenever the obsessional fears occurred. At the next session, Mrs. Fisher reported that she had practiced diligently and had had some degree of success during the first evening in reducing the frequency of her obsessional thoughts. However, the thoughts had remained at their original intensity for the remainder of the week. The therapist once again had Mrs. Fisher practice thought stopping in the office, and set the same homework assignment for her. However, she reported to the therapist the following week that the technique continued to be ineffective. At this point, the therapist decided to discontinue it, reasoning that the obsessional fears were being actively reinforced on an ongoing basis. Thus, it would presumably be necessary to identify what was maintaining the fearful thoughts and to effectively eliminate it before the fearful thoughts themselves could be eliminated.

Negative Self-Image

During these first sessions the therapist had also begun work on helping Mrs. Fisher to alter her negative beliefs about herself, and on helping her to receive and express anger appropriately. In order to alter Mrs. Fisher's negative beliefs about herself, the technique of cognitive rehearsal was employed. Mrs. Fisher was asked to formulate several statements about herself as a person that were as positive and complimentary as she could possibly believe, statements that she might be able to accept on one of her "good" days. Together Mrs. Fisher and the therapist formulated the following two sentences: "I am a competent woman and a good wife and mother," and "I am a capable and intelligent person and other people like and respect me." Next they searched for a pleasant activity that was a regular part of Mrs. Fisher's day and could serve as a reinforcer for these new adaptive thoughts. The activity selected was smoking a cigarette. The complete assignment was then assembled as follows. Mrs. Fisher was to select a time during the day when she very much felt like smoking a cigarette. She was then to write each sentence 20 times, repeating them to herself as she did so. When the writing task was completed, she was to follow it immediately by smoking a cigarette. Mrs. Fisher agreed to perform this assignment and did it for the three weeks as it was requested of her.

## Anger and Assertion

In order to gain information about events in Mrs. Fisher's daily life that were associated with angry feelings, the therapist asked her to keep systematic daily records showing each time she experienced an angry feeling, when and where it occurred, what else was happening at the time, and what, if anything, she did about it. The following week Mrs. Fisher brought in notes on no fewer than 29 situations in which she reported feeling angry. In some of these situations it would have been appropriate for her to be assertive without anger, and in some a direct expression of anger would have been the appropriate response.

**Assertiveness training.** The therapist approached the problem of nonassertiveness first because it seemed likely that many situations which currently aroused anger for Mrs. Fisher did so only because she had not been able to be assertive initially. Three typical examples of such situations taken from Mrs. Fisher's written observations were as follows. First, her son Peter had thrown a tantrum in a department store, and at another time had run uncontrollably around the store. She also felt very angry when it was likely that he would be successful at manipulating her to remain at nursery school with him. Second, a neighbor had called at 8:15 A.M. for advice about her daughter's cold sores. Apparently not satisfied, the neighbor showed up about four hours later accompanied by the daughter. Third, in regard to her husband, Mrs. Fisher reported two instances in which the car did not function properly and she felt strong anger at her husband for not having had it repaired. In each of these situations it was clear to the therapist that if Mrs. Fisher had been appropriately assertive when the situation had first arisen, she would have been much less likely to build up feelings of anger.

Mrs. Fisher also reported a number of other situations in which feelings of anger appeared to be quite appropriate and when a direct expression of anger would also have been appropriate. Almost all of these situations involved her husband. For example, despite her obvious need for help and support from him in managing Peter, he spent an entire day in the basement doing work for friends. On other occasions he would make a great deal of unnecessary noise early in the morning and would wake Peter, causing Mrs. Fisher extra work. Another situation that produced legitimate angry feelings was when she thought about her husband's accusations that there was never enough money and his implication that she was a spendthrift, when in reality she was very careful about money.

It is common for people to confuse anger with assertion, as Mrs. Fisher had done, and the next task for the behavior therapist was to clarify this for her and help her to differentiate between the two behaviors in her daily life. Assertion refers to expressing one's needs, opinions, and feelings directly. There usually is no reason for people to feel angry when they are being assertive because others usually respond positively when they are informed of a person's needs. Anger is often experienced when, as with Mrs. Fisher, there is a consistent expectation that one's needs will not be met and respected, or when people feel that their needs, feelings, or opinions are of little value to others.

The first step in teaching Mrs. Fisher to be more assertive was to identify a number of situations she had recently encountered, or would be likely to encounter, in which some form of assertiveness would be appropriate. The list of actual situations which Mrs. Fisher had recorded during the past week provided an excellent starting point. It is usual to arrange such a list in a hierarchy from the easiest to the most difficult for the patient. An alternative method of developing a hierarchy would be to take a single situation and to systematically vary the degree of assertiveness required. The latter approach was followed for Mrs. Fisher, and the assertiveness hierarchy was developed around a forthcoming situation for her: returning a recently purchased but unsuitable sweater to a large department store.

In constructing the hierarchy, the therapist paid particular attention to the specific cues which triggered Mrs. Fisher's unassertive behavior. The hierarchy was a graded series of scenarios containing an increasing number of these cues. For Mrs. Fisher the most important cues triggering unassertive behavior involved the degree to which her own needs were not accepted by the other person, as reflected in the content, tone, and general manner of the other person's response. Mrs. Fisher and the therapist together worked out six items in which the store clerk's response ranged from very accepting to very unaccepting. In each case, Mrs. Fisher was to go to the sweater counter of the department store and say to the clerk, "I'd like to return this sweater." The nature of the clerk's responses was to be as follows:

1. Clerk gives warm reassuring smile and accepts sweater immediately.
2. Clerk accepts sweater in a matter-of-fact manner.
3. Clerk is doubtful, but accepts sweater after discussion with Mrs. Fisher.
4. Clerk appears irritated and checks store's policy on returns before accepting sweater.
5. Clerk is clearly angry but eventually responds to Mrs. Fisher's calm insistence.
6. Clerk has angry outburst and refuses outright to accept sweater. Mrs. Fisher states that she will report incident to manager, and does so. Manager immediately accepts sweater and reprimands clerk.

For each of these items, the actual words to be used were spelled out. For example, in Item No. 1, it was agreed that the clerk would say: "Yes, certainly, ma'am. I can see the defect from here. Thank you for bringing it back. We want to be sure that our customers are fully satisfied." Each of the scenarios ended with the successful return of the sweater and with Mrs. Fisher walking away from the sweater counter putting the charge account refund receipt in her purse.

In teaching assertive skills in behavior therapy, two different procedures can initially be used: *imagery* and *role playing*. The use of imagery has already been discussed in Chapter 2. The patient is instructed to imagine vividly, like a daydream, the scenes that are worked out ahead of time. It is usual for the patient to be in a physically relaxed state, and the skills of relaxation and imagery are taught separately to the patient. In role playing, as in imagery, particular scenes are again worked out ahead of time. The therapist and patient act out the scene. The first time, the therapist plays the role of the patient, enabling the therapist to model appropriate ways for the patient to respond. Then the patient and therapist reverse roles, and the patient rehearses the appropriately assertive behavior that the therapist has constructed and modeled.

In working with Mrs. Fisher, the therapist used both imagery and role playing to teach assertive skills that she could use when encountering the store-clerk situation in real life. Such skills can, of course, also be used productively in other situations. In other words, the therapist also encourages the patient to *generalize* these new adaptive behaviors. With Mrs. Fisher, the therapist had chosen to begin assertive training with a situation that was not one of the most difficult for her, but rather represented a manageable first step. As the therapist predicted, Mrs. Fisher was successful in learning assertiveness in this initial situation through imagery and then applying it in real life.

The therapist next had Mrs. Fisher rehearse in imagery several additional situations involving the appropriate expression of assertiveness, most of them involving her husband. However, Mrs. Fisher was not yet told to try out these behaviors in real life, since the therapist felt that this could best be initiated in working with the Fishers together in the therapy office.

**Expressing anger appropriately.** Before working with the Fishers together, the therapist gave Mrs. Fisher some similar training dealing with the appropriate expression of anger. Once again, a number of situations were employed for training purposes, each involving a graded sequence in which progressively more and more cues triggering anger were present. A typical problem situation was that Mr. Fisher consistently ignored his wife at home. He habitually spent almost all his time either reading the newspaper, watching TV, or doing projects for friends. The therapist first worked with Mrs. Fisher to help her clarify and articulate these strong, but poorly verbalized, feelings about Mr. Fisher's behavior. Her anger was intensified by the fact that she relied heavily on her husband for adult interaction since her problems prevented her from getting much interaction elsewhere. It should be noted that prior to this stage of therapy Mrs. Fisher's only skill for eliciting attention from her husband under such circumstances was to throw an hysterical tantrum and threaten suicide.

While listening to Mrs. Fisher, the therapist formulated coherent ways in which she might express her angry feelings. When a sufficient number of verbalizations had been worked out, Mrs. Fisher and the therapist role-played a discussion between the Fishers in which the therapist, playing Mrs. Fisher, calmly asked her husband to engage in a serious discussion with her, and then told him coherently of her angry feelings and the reasons for them. As the role playing progressed, it became clear to Mrs. Fisher that her husband would not be likely to tolerate such a discussion, but would probably become very defensive and would terminate the situation by physically withdrawing from it. Therefore, the therapist asked to see the Fishers together once again in order to facilitate their joint communication skills.

At this stage in the therapy, after six sessions, Mrs. Fisher had been assisted in comfortably and appropriately expressing her anger at a variety of people, most prominently her husband, within the safety of the therapeutic situation. Because some of the give and take in the imagery and role playing involved receiving as well as expressing anger, she had also learned to accept anger without feeling so devastated.

**Communicating with husband.** The therapist asked Mr. and Mrs. Fisher to select examples of situations in which she became angry at him and situations in which he became angry with her. Then they worked together in formulating an acceptable way for Mrs. Fisher to express anger about a particular situation without making him extremely defensive. The therapist helped each of them to formulate the specific words that would actually be used in the interaction (e.g., "I didn't realize I was leaving you alone, but when I come home from work you tend to immediately dump your problems on me, and I need a little time to relax because I am having a hard time at work right now").

One of their homework assignments was to read *The Intimate Enemy* by George R. Bach and Peter Wyden, which discusses constructive and destructive ways for handling anger within a marital relationship. They were also instructed to watch for the occurrence at home of the situations that they had rehearsed in the therapy office, and to try to handle them in the way that had been rehearsed.

As already noted, it was clear that to the therapist Mrs. Fisher's hysterical outbursts followed periods of inattention from Mr. Fisher, and that they were her only effective, though highly destructive, means of getting him to interact with her. In order to modify this behavior it was necessary to help them set up adaptive interactions that both would enjoy. One such situation was sitting down in the evening for coffee and conversation. To plan for this, the therapist helped Mr. Fisher to rearrange his evening plans in order to make time for this interaction. The therapist then had the Fishers agree on a specific time each evening during the coming week when this interaction would actually take place. The therapist also instructed Mr. Fisher in how to handle his wife's hysterical outbursts. At such times, Mr. Fisher was to tell her firmly to call the therapist on the telephone and then to walk out of the room. In summary, the therapist arranged for Mr. Fisher to provide his wife with a positive means of getting attention and affection, and for him to ignore her unadaptive ways of seeking attention. The Fishers were also asked to keep notes on these interactions during the week.

**Managing Peter.** At the next session, the ninth, Mr. and Mrs. Fisher reported that they had engaged in the planned interaction on five out of seven days, and that they were much more satisfied with their relationship. The therapist encouraged the Fishers to continue with these new behaviors and then began teaching Mrs. Fisher how to be appropriately assertive with Peter. First, they identified situations where an assertive stance would be appropriate for Mrs. Fisher. These included Peter's running around a department store out of Mrs. Fisher's control, and his whining and fussing for attention. Together they agreed upon appropriate ways for Mrs. Fisher to respond, and the therapist had her systematically rehearse them in imagery. As a homework assignment for that week she agreed to keep observational notes on her actual responses to these situations whenever they occurred. It should be noted that, as with Mrs. Fisher's own negative attention-seeking behavior, the therapist had to ensure that a positive means of getting attention was available to Peter before his maladaptive means could be successfully discouraged.

## Mrs. Fisher's Obsessional Fears

Attention was now focused on Mrs. Fisher's fearful obsessions. The therapist predicted that these fears should by now have diminished somewhat if they were being cued or maintained by her anger, by inattention from Mr. Fisher, or by lack of adaptive skills in handling Peter. Surprisingly, however, the fearful obsessions were as strong as ever, and the therapist concluded that they were associated with a set of events which had not as yet been identified. In the tenth session, therefore, the therapist met with Mr. and Mrs. Fisher together and reviewed the history of the disorder in detail. Mrs. Fisher's personal history was also reviewed. In addition, Mrs. Fisher had brought in her first set of daily observational notes describing situations in which her fearful obsessions occurred and the events associated with them.

**Fears of death and sickness.** These different sources of information now left little doubt that the central focus of Mrs. Fisher's disorder involved cues of death and also sickness. Mrs. Fisher initially denied that she was concerned in any way with these topics. The therapist persisted despite her denials, and spent four full sessions exploring present and past feelings, thoughts, and situations associated with death. It appeared to the therapist that the original learning experience involving this constellation of cues was her father's death when she was eight years old. Over these several sessions, Mrs. Fisher was gradually able to express more and more clearly her strong fearful belief that she had actually caused her father's death by her thoughts just before he died ("I'm afraid that Daddy's going to die."). The therapist also helped Mrs. Fisher to identify her long-standing characteristic way of attempting to cope with anxiety-laden situations by perceiving herself to be in full control of them.

During these four weeks, the therapist persuaded Mrs. Fisher to engage in extensive discussions with her family about the formerly taboo topic of her father's death many years ago. Her family members responded with a new willingness to explore this topic, and she spent a considerable amount of time talking with her mother and looking at old pictures. Another homework assignment was to visit her father's grave, which Mrs. Fisher had not done since soon after the funeral. Peter accompanied Mrs. Fisher to the cemetery and asked many questions about his grandfather, which Mrs. Fisher answered fully and well. Through these new activities involving her father's death, Mrs. Fisher was systematically desensitized in real life rather than imagery to her fear of this topic. She had also gained a great deal of new information about it, which helped her see it in its proper perspective within her life.

The therapist next addressed Mrs. Fisher's current fears involving sickness and death. As the reader may recall, Mrs. Fisher had suffered a "nervous breakdown" when her husband and Peter had both become sick at the same time. Discussion with Mrs. Fisher revealed that the strongest fear of sickness and death for Mrs. Fisher was evoked by sickness in an immediate family member. Three different problems were involved here for Mrs. Fisher: (a) her extreme anxiety in response to these cues; (b) her lack of adaptive skills in handling such situations, and (c) her irrational beliefs about her anxiety, which prevented her from recognizing that illness in close family members constituted perhaps the strongest anxiety-arousing cues for her.

The therapist approached the task of anxiety reduction by systematic desensitization in imagery, which was described in Chapter 2 and again will be in Chapter 4. The hierarchy was a graded series of situations involving illness in the family, from mildly anxiety arousing to intensely anxiety arousing. In order to rehearse new and appropriate ways for Mrs. Fisher to respond in situations involving sickness or death, she and the therapist together identified the ways in which people normally behave in such situations. Some of this material was presented for Mrs. Fisher to rehearse in imagery, and some of it was incorporated into homework assignments for her to rehearse in real life.

**Changing irrational thinking.** The most important aspect of this phase of treatment involved changing Mrs. Fisher's irrational beliefs about the sources of her anxiety. The therapist emphasized the connection between her anxiety and cues of sickness. This originated from the time of her father's death, when she and her sisters were sent to stay at an aunt's house while her father was hospitalized. She remembered believing at that time that if only she had stayed with her father, she might have been able to save him. Mrs. Fisher's faulty thinking was vividly illustrated during one session when she reported that her fears had increased during the week and believed that this increase was triggered by Peter's behavior. An extended discussion revealed that Mrs. Fisher had learned during the week that her mother had cancer! The increase in her fearful obsessions dated from exactly that time, along with an increase in general anxiety. When Peter experienced some difficulties in kindergarten the following day, Mrs. Fisher attributed her fears and anxiety to this situation, instead of recognizing the devastating effect the news of her mother's serious illness had on her and dealing with it directly.

During the same therapy session Mrs. Fisher suddenly remembered for the first time that two weeks before her father suffered his stroke, her mother told him that he was acting as though he did not feel well and insisted that he see a prominent and "competent" doctor for a complete checkup. He had done so, and the doctor had given him a clean bill of health. Mrs. Fisher also recalled saying to herself at that time that she must be the only person who was competent to look after him, since she would not have allowed such a stupid mistake to be made. Such an event obviously contributed to her present irrational beliefs in this area, and to her tendency to perceive herself as being in control of matters at anxiety-producing times. By the end of these four sessions, Mrs. Fisher was still somewhat fearful of cues related to sickness and death but had changed her irrational beliefs about the source of her anxiety. She now said that she was willing to cope directly with these anxiety-arousing cues, and the therapist informed her that she possessed the necessary knowledge and skills to do so. That is, she began to respond to cues of illness in the family just as any other person would.

Mrs. Fisher had now recognized that her high anxiety was in major part a response to cues of sickness (and potential death) in close family members. She accepted the therapist's statement that her obsessional thoughts were a response to this anxiety, rather than the cause of it, although she did not understand how this could be so. She had also learned to recognize cues of sickness when they occurred and to respond to them with appropriate and normal thoughts and actions. The therapist helped Mrs. Fisher to prepare some adaptive self-statements to make when these anxiety-producing events occurred; for example, "Peter has a cold, and although it's uncomfortable for him now, he'll soon be fine."

Mrs. Fisher's obsessional fears had now diminished somewhat but were still quite significant for her, and she still had an extremely restricted life. Because Mrs. Fisher now appeared to possess adequate skills in responding adaptively to the cues that had been triggering them, the therapist decided that she was now ready to take active steps to systematically eliminate the abnormal behaviors which were formerly the result of her obsessional fears and were so disruptive to a normal life. In considering which specific behaviors to work on first, the therapist noted that Mrs. Fisher never committed any of the harmful acts that she was fearful of doing. However, her husband played a part in reinforcing her fear that she would commit a harmful act by collaborating in locking up the so-called dangerous items and keeping the key in his possession. Another way in which he reinforced her problem was to agree to little or no social life, although both wished for more.

**"Declassifying" feared objects.** Since Mrs. Fisher felt that she was a "dangerous person," the therapist introduced the word "classified" to refer to those items and behaviors which marked her as dangerous. At the next session, the seventeenth, the therapist explained to Mr. and Mrs. Fisher that they were going to slowly and systematically "declassify" all these aspects of Mrs. Fisher's life, and began to negotiate with them as to which ones to declassify first. In technical terms, since Mrs. Fisher had now learned adaptive ways of responding to anxiety-producing cues, the therapist planned to assist her in extinguishing the unadaptive response, that is, the obsessional thoughts and the highly restrictive behaviors by which she sought to control the obsessions. This was to be done by exposing her, in real life, to the objects and events that she was fearful of and to demonstrate that she could cope with them normally.

As a first step, the therapist prepared a list of all the classified items, and Mrs. Fisher agreed to declassify three items per week. The first week she selected the bottle of children's vitamins, adult vitamins, and a decongestant, and together with her husband she selected a new place in the house to keep these items. At the next session she reported initially experiencing some anxiety, but she had soon forgotten about the items and had gone through the week without additional stress. After six weeks, all the so-called dangerous items were declassified and fully available to her in the house. This provided its own reinforcement because Mrs. Fisher could now take aspirin immediately if she had a headache during the day, instead of waiting for her husband to come home to unlock the cupboard. She was also proud of being able to perform this behavior without the anxiety that she had come to expect over the past few years.

In order to declassify social situations, the therapist asked the Fishers to prepare a list of situations which they either would be required to engage in or wanted to engage in. These items were then arranged in a hierarchy of graded steps, from least anxiety-arousing to most anxiety-arousing. During each week of the declassification period, the therapist negotiated with Mr. and Mrs. Fisher to engage in one or two items on the hierarchy.

At this point in the therapy, it became clear that Mrs. Fisher had learned to habitually respond with obsessional thoughts to a whole range of different anxieties in addition to anxiety over sickness and death. She would mistakenly believe that it was the obsessional thought that caused the anxiety that she experienced and would immediately do something to try to remove the obsessional thought, for example, lock up the aspirin or refrain from visiting her neighbor. At this point in therapy, Mrs. Fisher became progressively more adept at recognizing the particular cues that triggered anxiety whenever she became anxious. And with her new skills she was able to respond directly to those cues and reduce the anxiety, rather than responding with obsessional thoughts and then making futile attempts to reduce the obsessional thoughts.

## Generalizing Adaptive Behaviors

In sessions 23 through 27, the therapist helped Mrs. Fisher to increase her adaptive behavior in a variety of situations and also to maintain all the new behaviors which she had learned. Typically, she would report to the therapist events which represented marked changes from her former functioning, involving new behaviors and diminished obsessional thoughts. She would also report instances in which she had had difficulty engaging in adaptive behavior or where she had continued to experience obsessional thoughts to a troublesome degree. She and the therapist would examine the situations together and would attempt to identify anxiety cues that she had missed to help her work out appropriate responses to new situations. Included here were visits to her gynecologist and pediatrician without the presence of another adult, and discussion with her husband about having a second child.

In session 28, the final session, the therapist met with Mr. and Mrs. Fisher together to review the changes that each of them had made. The therapist stressed once again for Mrs. Fisher that her obsessional thoughts were triggered by cues of sickness and death and to a lesser extent by any strong anxiety-arousing cue. The therapist also reviewed forthcoming situations for which Mrs. Fisher had significant fear, such as Peter's beginning regular school. Mrs. Fisher was not "cured" at this point; however, the therapist believed that she now possessed the necessary skills to cope adaptively with new problem situations, and that she and her husband would continue to improve their relationship and their communication. A four-month follow-up showed that Peter had begun school without incident, and that Mr. and Mrs. Fisher had purchased a new home, of which they were very proud. Mrs. Fisher had taken responsibility for selling the old home and was extremely pleased with the assertiveness she showed in this venture. At a one-year follow-up, Mrs. Fisher reported experiencing a sense of peace and well-being that she had not felt for years. She had handled highly feared situations satisfactorily, such as when Peter came home from school with diarrhea and vomiting. She reported still having occasional obsessional thoughts, but she was able to handle them satisfactorily and without disrupting her daily activities.

# 4

# Common Clinical Problems

In this chapter we discuss the behavioral treatment of several common and important problems for which people often seek help from mental health professionals and from physicians. The problems discussed here are ones which people tend to see as residing "inside" themselves rather than involving interactions with other people. In most instances, however, these problems do indeed involve significant interaction with others. First, we discuss one of the most common problems for which people seek help from mental health personnel: *unmanageable anxiety*, and difficulties stemming from it. A related group of difficulties is *psychosomatic disorders*, such as certain aspects of asthma and headache. The uses of *biofeedback* technology in behavioral treatment are also identified.

Last, we discuss behavioral contributions to the understanding and treatment of *depression*. It should be noted that although a patient may complain of several of these problems at the same time, the behavior therapist would usually approach each as a separate and distinct difficulty and would not assume they are related unless his observations indicate that this is the case.

## Anxiety

Anxiety is perhaps the most pervasive psychological problem afflicting civilized people. The concept of anxiety figures prominently in every major theory of psychological disorder, and in some theories it is regarded as the most basic problem from which all other problems arise.

We do not overlook the fact that perfectly well-adjusted people are often anxious, and that there are many things in the world to be realistically anxious about. Also, there are times when a certain amount of anxiety has positive benefits, motivating people to do a great variety of things that need to be done: getting the car fixed, paying the rent, taking care of bodily complaints, and studying for exams. In this chapter we are, of course, concerned with dysfunctional anxiety, that is, anxiety which disrupts a person's normal functioning.

Behavioral scientists view anxiety as an automatic reaction to anticipated punishment, pain, or other aversive events. A sure way to generate anxiety in people is to do something aversive to them and then threaten them with more aversiveness. Under these circumstances, practically all persons respond automatically with anxiety and will learn new behaviors to avoid additional anxiety. Further, and this is most important for the development of future problems, the anxiety and the avoidance behavior become conditioned to the cues of the original aversive conditioning situation. Thereafter, these cues retain the ability to elicit anxiety even if the actual aversive event rarely occurs. For example, a child who is chased and bitten by a dog may become fearful at the sight of dogs, and perhaps also other animals that look like dogs, because of an original conditioning experience with a particular dog. Here, the cues to which anxiety is conditioned could include the sight of a dog, its bark, and more importantly, thoughts about dogs (for example, "It's going to bite me"), since frightening thoughts are cues that are often present in the original learning experience.

It is a curious phenomenon that people can continue to be made anxious by cues for many years after the impending "danger" or aversive event that is signaled by the cues has completely disappeared. Behavioral scientists believe that this is because people learn to automatically avoid things (that is, cues) that make them anxious, including *thoughts* about anxiety-producing events. In other words, people are often motivated to be unaware of the actual cues that trigger their anxiety and are therefore unable to do anything constructive about decreasing the anxiety. In fact, the majority of patients with chronic neurotic anxiety problems have little or no idea about what is making them anxious. However, because it is natural for people to provide themselves with explanations for what they do, such people have a "cover story" by which they explain to themselves why they are anxious.

The behavior therapist's task is to enlist the patient's aid as a careful observer in tracking down the actual cues that elicit the anxiety. The reader will remember that although Mrs. Fisher was unaware initially that fears of death or sickness of loved ones were cueing and maintaining her high level of anxiety and restricting her activities, she and the therapist were able to track this down, together with the probable circumstances of original learning. It is usually not necessary to know the original learning circumstances in order to bring about a change in current functioning, however. Let us again remind the reader that cues triggering anxiety may be overt, such as a person or a place, or they may be covert, such as thoughts or specific "feelings." Let us also emphasize again that anxiety always occurs in response to a specific cue, even if the patient has no idea that he is responding to a cue or flatly denies that this is the case.

It is often true that the original cues to which anxiety was conditioned are no longer present in the person's environment. In this case, the behavior therapist will suspect that the cues to which the person is responding may be thoughts and will give the patient careful instructions in doing the behavioral observations to keep a record of thoughts that are present immediately before the anxiety occurs. These thoughts are often fleeting, so that it may at first be difficult for the patient to develop any consistent record. However, the patient will be encouraged to persevere and will often be successful in identifying the cueing thoughts.

People experience anxiety in different ways. Perhaps the most universal experience is the characteristic feeling of "butterflies-in-the-stomach." Essentially, this is a physiological change involving an increased secretion of adrenalin. Different people describe it in different words, but everyone agrees that it is most unpleasant, and the almost universal response is to try to escape from it when it occurs and avoid it in the future.

Anxiety also involves other physiological changes. Heart rate can increase, sweating and trembling can occur, the knees can knock together, the mouth can go dry, throat and other muscles can tighten up, blood can drain from the face, and feelings of nausea can occur. People differ in the extent to which each of these behaviors takes place, and for any specific individual perhaps most of them will not occur. However, sometimes one of them is, in fact, the basic focus of a person's problem. An example would be tightening of the throat muscles at the same time as one is trying to eat, or the occurrence of nausea and vomiting in social situations. When people develop problems that center around one particular physiological change associated with anxiety, they often fail to recognize the other aspects of anxiety. Also, they often perceive the anxiety as caused by the physiological difficulty and are quite unaware of what is really cueing their anxiety. Thus, a woman who sought help for involuntary choking when attempting to eat in social situations perceived herself as having no other anxieties apart from social discomfort, which she believed was caused by her choking.

A third aspect of anxiety is interference with the ability to think, concentrate, and remember; in other words, interference with cognitive activities. Many people complain of "going blank" during an important examination, or find that when trying to study they are just "watching the words" and not actively reading and comprehending. Cognitive difficulties associated with anxiety can also be seen in people who find that a stream of irrelevant thoughts and worries constantly circulates through their heads, preventing them from focusing productively at the task at hand. Sometimes individuals will seek professional help especially for these cognitive problems caused by anxiety. For such a problem, the behavior therapist would once again search for the cues triggering the anxiety and the resulting difficulties in thinking or concentration.

### Tension

In order to design a treatment strategy for a person complaining of anxiety, the behavior therapist will not only try to identify what is cueing and maintaining the anxiety but will also look to see how the person experiences the anxiety, such as in unpleasant feelings, physiological difficulties, cognitive disruption, or perhaps as some combination of these problems. One of the words commonly used in connection with anxiety and psychological distress is "tension." Because this word is the source of much confusion, let us clarify its meaning. In the context of mental health problems, the word tension is used rather indiscriminately to refer to either (a) excessive physical or muscle tension; (b) cognitive difficulties associated with anxiety, such as worry or inability to concentrate; or (c) some combination of the two. The behavior therapist approaches the problem of excessive physical tension by training the person in physical relaxation procedures, described later in this chapter. Cognitive difficulties are treated quite differently, using cognitively oriented procedures also illustrated later in this chapter.

Because of the confusion in the use of the word "tension," there has been an unfortunate tendency to use physical relaxation as a treatment for cognitive difficulties. This is simply an instance of a therapist trying a technique without understanding the technology. The confusion has also led to the development of inappropriate terms such as "relaxation therapy," which is said to be a treatment for "nervous tension" or "being uptight." Similarly, the term "biofeedback therapy" has now made its appearance. Biofeedback, a set of experimental procedures to be discussed below, has nothing to do with changing cognitive difficulties, but has captivated would-be behavior therapists with its scientific appearance and electronic equipment. Legitimate uses of biofeedback technology in behavior therapy are discussed later in this chapter. It should be emphasized that *tension* in the context of behavioral psychology refers only to physical or muscle tension.

## Treatment of Anxiety

The most effective behavioral procedure for treating anxiety by behavior therapy is through *desensitization,* the systematic and persistent exposure to the cues that trigger anxiety, but without the feared consequences occurring. Often consequences that are pleasant for the patient are deliberately arranged instead. As indicated in Chapter 2, this procedure is termed "extinction," or if new, pleasant consequences are arranged, the term "counterconditioning" is used.

In accordance with this plan, the behavior therapist must first deal with two aspects of the problem: he must identify any current reinforcers that are actively maintaining the anxiety and must arrange for their removal; and he must work with the patient in identifying the cues that trigger the anxiety. Sometimes the cues and/or reinforcers are easily and readily identified, and the problem becomes one of simple reexposure to the feared cues under therapeutic conditions. Sometimes, the majority of the therapeutic time is used in simply trying to identify the cues triggering the anxiety, and/or in working toward removal of the reinforcers by negotiation if they are interpersonal in nature, or by cognitive relearning if they consist of destructive self-statements.

## Removing the Reinforcers

As stated above, trying to remove the events that are reinforcing the anxiety may occupy a good portion of the therapeutic time. In Mrs. Fisher's case, for example, some of these events were cognitive, involving irrational beliefs, and some were interpersonal, mainly involving her husband. Mr. Fisher was unwittingly playing a significant part in maintaining his wife's anxieties by agreeing with her that she was a dangerous person and by locking up "dangerous" substances away from her reach. Not only did this reinforce Mrs. Fisher's obsessional beliefs that she was dangerous, but it also perpetuated her anxiety in another very common way. It enabled her to avoid exposure to the cues associated with the anxiety, namely, medicines and other substances that could poison people. The most destructive result of avoiding what is believed to be triggering the anxiety, or course, is that one never gets the opportunity to learn that the feared consequences do not occur.

## Discovering the Cues

With some anxiety **pro**blems the cues triggering the anxiety are known by the patient and can be immediately identified. In many simple phobias, for example, the patient really is afraid of snakes, or public speaking, or flying in airplanes, or expressing anger. At other times, however, the cues that the patient believes to be the source of the anxiety are not the real ones. In Mrs. Fisher's case, for example, the real cues were sickness and death, and it took the therapist and patient some time to identify them. Mrs. Fisher thought that the cues were medicines and poisons. The therapist initially thought that the cues were whatever made her feel angry, most often her husband. If the behavior therapist systematically exposes the patient to the cues that are presumed to trigger the anxiety, without the feared consequences, and the anxiety does not diminish, then those are not cues triggering the anxiety.

Sometimes the therapist is not able to identify the cues specifically, but can identify the general situation that appears to contain the cues. The patient, for example, might know with certainty that his chronic anxiety is highest whenever he visits his parents, but he might not know what the triggering cues are in that general situation. However, such partial information is often sufficient for the therapist to begin systematic exposure, which would usually be done in imagery. The use of imagery would enable the therapist to rapidly expose the patient to a number of different situations at his parents' home and perhaps to gain more information about the specific cues that are triggering the anxiety. In imaginal work, unexpected thoughts sometimes occur which help to identify the real anxiety cues. For example, when the therapist was having Mrs. Fisher imagine herself at her son's nursery school, a situation in which her fearful obsessions occurred, she suddenly realized that she was fearful lest the nursery school teachers would not be able to control the children, and that some harm might therefore come to her son. This led Mrs. Fisher and the therapist closer to recognizing the real cues for anxiety; namely, sickness or other harm occurring to people that were important to her in situations which were not in her control.

### Systematic Exposure

The core of the anxiety reduction process in behavior therapy is systematic planned exposure to the cues triggering the anxiety, under conditions when the feared consequences do not occur. There are a number of ways of carrying out this procedure. For example, it can be done in a series of small, graded steps over a period of time, or it can be done in one big step, a procedure referred to as "flooding" or "implosion." Flooding, while often quicker than graded exposure, tends to be unpleasant for most patients. Either procedure can be conducted using imaginal cues or real-life cues, or some combination of both.

In Mrs. Fisher's case, the therapist exposed her to sickness and death cues by systematically having her discuss her father's death, visit his grave, explore her father's death with her extended family, and look at old pictures. The therapist also had the patient reexperience her father's death in imagery, and had her engage in carefully graded imaginal experiences in which both her husband and her son became sick and died. Since some fear had also become conditioned to the items which Mrs. Fisher had "classified," she was systematically exposed to these cues also. The reader will recall that "declassification," or extinction of anxiety, associated with these cues proceeded quite rapidly once the reinforcers for the anxiety (her husband's behavior and her own destructive self-statements) had been removed.

## Case Example of Desensitization

We now describe a simple and straightforward case of treatment of a specific fear through desensitization. The patient, Mrs. Walters, was in her mid-forties and had been terrified of thunderstorms for some 25 years. During the summer months, when thunderstorms were more frequent, she would begin each day by listening to the early-morning weather forecast on at least two TV channels. Next she would call the local weather service, and then she would begin her day-long series of inspections of the sky. On days when there was no possibility of rain, she would be happy and relieved, but the slightest possibility of a thundershower caused her to revise her plans for the entire day in order to avoid being alone or caught in the rain.

Examination of the daily records kept by Mrs. Walters over a two-week period, plus an extended interview with her husband, failed to identify any obvious events that were actively reinforcing Mrs. Walters' fear and her avoidance behavior. It also appeared likely that the real anxiety cues were indeed thunderstorms, cloudy skies, and rain. The therapist therefore decided to go ahead with systematic graded exposure to these cues. For convenience, it was decided to first conduct this exposure in imagery, and then to negotiate with Mrs. Walters to expose herself to the real-life cues as her anxiety diminished and as these cues were produced by the weather.

Several half-hour periods were spent teaching Mrs. Walters how to quickly achieve a complete state of physical relaxation, in the expectation that this would enhance the intensity of her imagery. Several further half-hour periods were spent teaching her how to engage in vivid fantasies. Mrs. Walters practiced both the imagery and the relaxation skills at home in accordance with the homework assignments which the therapist set for her. The next step was the construction of a fear hierarchy, and in fact three hierarchies were developed, each devoted to a slightly different set of cues. Some of the items from each hierarchy are listed in Table 4.1, ordered from least to most fear-arousing.

Table 4.1
Selected Items from Three Fear Hierarchies
Used in the Desensitization of Anxiety Thunderstorms

| Subject | Selected Items |
| --- | --- |
| Morning TV weather forecasts | 1. Hearing that the weather will be perfect, with no chance of rain.<br>5. Hearing that there will be cloudy skies, with some possibility of rain.<br>10. Hearing that there will be a major thunderstorm during the afternoon. |
| Looking out of the window at home | 1. Seeing a perfect, blue sky.<br>4. Seeing half blue sky, half white clouds.<br>7. Seeing a gray, overcast sky.<br>9. Seeing a very dark patch of clouds that seem to be getting darker. |
| Miscellaneous, away from home | 3. Seeing a slight drizzle while driving home from the supermarket.<br>7. Feeling a slight drizzle when getting out of the car to go into the supermarket.<br>10. Seeing heavy rain out of the office window while at work.<br>15. Driving on a strange highway during a thunderstorm. |

The actual desensitization procedure was begun by having Mrs. Walters become completely relaxed in a reclining chair, and then having her imagine vividly the lowest item on the first fear hierarchy. If she experienced the slightest anxiety, she was instructed to raise a finger, whereupon the therapist would tell her to dismiss the fantasy and devote her attention to improving her state of relaxation. After two successive presentations of an item for 15 or 20 seconds during which no anxiety was experienced, the next item on the hierarchy was presented. The entire procedure took 12 one-hour sessions, and during the last session she was able to experience the vivid fantasy of driving through a violent thunderstorm without the slightest feeling of discomfort.

At the beginning of the sixth session, Mrs. Walters reported feeling less concerned after having heard a weather forecast that predicted rain. The therapist therefore instructed her to begin keeping a written record of her feelings after each daily forecast, and to say to herself during the forecast: "It doesn't really matter whether it rains or not." At this time, the therapist also negotiated with her to start exposing herself to the fear cues in real life by going outside on overcast days and also by watching any rain through her window. Mrs. Walters was able to systematically increase her exposure week by week, and she received a great deal of enthusiastic approval from her family for this new behavior. By the final session she was deliberately going outside during threatening weather, had entirely ceased listening to weather forecasts, and was looking forward to the next major thunderstorm so that she could adequately test her newly acquired freedom from panic. A follow-up inquiry after one year showed that these fears were no longer a part of Mrs. Walters' life.

## Physical Tension and Muscle Relaxation

Ever since 1929, when physiologist Edmund Jacobson published a book on the thesis that neurotic anxieties could be cured through systematic muscle relaxation, the topic of muscle tension and relaxation has been closely associated with the topic of anxiety. While there is no good evidence that anxiety can be reduced simply by muscle relaxation, there are a number of ways in which muscle relaxation can be utilized productively by the behavior therapist. One that we have already discussed, and perhaps the most common, is its use to enhance the effectiveness of imaginal procedures for reducing anxiety and learning new behaviors.

A second use of muscle relaxation is with people who are physically tense, and who find that their tension causes significant discomfort and interference with their daily activities. Because muscle relaxation is relatively simple to learn and can be engaged in to some extent at almost any time, the behavior therapist usually teaches tense people to develop a schedule for relaxing at set times during the day, and also teaches them to recognize when they are particularly tense. Such people often have difficulty going to sleep at night, and the ability to relax systematically and completely is also useful in increasing the probability of falling asleep.

A third use of muscle relaxation in behavior therapy is with problems that specifically involve excessive muscle tension in certain parts of the body. Tension headaches, for example, involve excessive muscle tension in certain muscle groups of the head, neck, and/or shoulders. Patients with tension headaches tend to tense these muscle groups without being aware of doing so. A central part of the behavior therapist's procedure is to systematically teach them to tense and relax until they become aware of their degree of tension in these muscles and can relax them voluntarily. It should be emphasized that some patients may be receiving active reinforcement for their headaches, such as attention from a spouse, or the termination of nagging. The therapist must search for and remove such reinforcers before the patient is likely to be successful in eliminating the headaches voluntarily through relaxation training.

Other problems in which muscle tension plays a central role include tics, stuttering, excessive tightness of the chest and throat, vaginismus (excessive muscle contractions of the vagina), and some forms of low back pain. Essentially any muscle group in the body can be involved in a problem of excessive physical tension, depending on the particular learning history of the individual and on predisposing factors which are not well understood at the present time.

**Teaching muscle relaxation.** The teaching of muscle relaxation skills generally follows a standardized procedure, and is assisted by daily practice over one or more weeks depending on the person. Some persons can learn muscle relaxation directly from a record or tape recording, several of which are available commercially. Relaxation training is also commonly used in other fields of endeavor, such as in Lamaze training for natural childbirth, in Yoga, and in training exercises for dancing and gymnastics. The therapist or instructor usually begins relaxation training by having the person recline or lie down with eyes closed. The person is told to tense a particular body part, such as the hand, and then gradually relax it, paying close attention to the behavior and the feelings involved. This procedure is repeated systematically for all major parts of the body, and each time the person is encouraged to achieve a more and more complete level of relaxation. Full instructions are available in more advanced texts on the practice of behavior therapy. Complete muscle relaxation usually brings with it characteristic feelings of either floating or sinking, and sometimes sleepiness. For many people, there is an increased awareness of internal bodily feelings and a heightened ability to fantasize or daydream.

## Treating Cognitive Difficulties

Just as some people tend to develop a problem around a particular physiological aspect of anxiety, so others tend to develop problems around a particular cognitive aspect of anxiety. Let us now examine a case in which the therapist employed competing thoughts to replace unadaptive thoughts which were generated by anxiety and were interfering with ongoing activity. Jack, a 19-year-old college student, sought help for his difficulties in concentrating while trying to study. Jack complained that he just "watched the words" without comprehending them, and his determined attempts to focus on the content of the material would result in his mind wandering off altogether. He was convinced that his basic problem was an inability to concentrate, and he believed that the strong anxiety which he experienced was caused by his study difficulties. During the initial interview, the therapist noted that Jack had achieved satisfactory grades in high school, and suggested that other cues, of which Jack was not currently aware, might be triggering the anxiety.

The therapist asked Jack to keep a record of his thoughts while trying to study during the following week. These records showed that Jack's most persistent thought was something like the following: "I'll never be able to learn this; it's just too hard for me." The therapist introduced an incompatible self-statement which Jack was to write out 50 times per day, and to repeat silently whenever he felt anxious while studying: "I can learn my college material just like anybody else." The next week Jack reported that this new self-statement had triggered the persistent thought that his father and older brother had not been able to satisfactorily complete their college work and had often told Jack that college would be too difficult for him also. Here was a possible more basic source of anxiety for Jack. Sympathetic questioning by the therapist revealed that Jack believed that he was in danger of triggering a serious family conflict, which could be avoided only if Jack told himself that he could not manage college work and if he proceeded to fulfill this belief.

The therapist persuaded Jack to bring the matter up with his father, and Jack found that his fears of family conflict were groundless. Now that the consequences maintaining Jack's fearful thoughts were removed, Jack found it easy to continue the adaptive self-statements. His anxiety diminished, and he found that he was able to study in a normal manner, as he had done during high school. To summarize, Jack's "poor concentration" turned out to be a product of interfering thoughts, and his anxiety was triggered by these interfering thoughts rather than by his inability to study. The therapist located and dealt with the events that were reinforcing the interfering thoughts (avoidance of anxiety over a family conflict), and then helped the patient directly extinguish the thoughts and normalize his study behavior.

## Physical and Psychosomatic Problems

In this section we introduce the behavioral treatment of psychological problems that result in a *physical* difficulty. A partial list of such difficulties for which behavior therapy has had some degree of success would include hysterical blindness and deafness, anorexia nervosa (inability to eat), certain forms of headache, psychogenic choking and gagging, ulcers, writer's cramp, chronic pain, and some cases of skin disorder, asthma, and epilepsy. One other major area, problems in normal sexual functioning, is discussed separately in Chapter 6.

Some of these difficulties, such as ulcers, involve an obvious physical problem, while for others, such as hysterical deafness, there is no observable physical change. The term "hysteria" or "conversion hysteria" has traditionally been used to classify problems in which no physical change occurs. Their cases are sufficiently unusual as to attract considerable attention, but they are actually quite rare nowadays. In such cases, although no physical reason can be found for the problem, the remainder of the person's life circumstances shows that obvious anxiety is avoided by having the problem. Such people are convinced that their problem is a physical one, however, and are generally quite unreceptive to psychological treatment. The therapist's main task is to persuade the patient to stay in treatment long enough so that the source of anxiety can be identified and the patient can be taught new, adaptive ways of responding to the situation.

Far more common are *psychosomatic* or *psychophysiological* problems in which there are definite physical changes that are at least partly generated and maintained by learning procedures. These changes may either be temporary, such as with a headache based on excessive muscle tension, or permanent, such as an ulcer. In practice there is some degree of overlap between the two areas "hysterical" and "psychosomatic," and behavioral scientists do not yet have a full understanding as to how many of these disorders come about.

For a case to be regarded as "pure" hysteria, psychological factors would have to be entirely responsible for the problem. In most cases, however, there appears to be a physical weakness or predisposition which is magnified by learning processes. Recent research on asthma, for example, showed that asthma sufferers responded with bronchial constriction when an allergenic substance was introduced. However, they also showed some asthmatic constriction when a cue was introduced that had been present with the allergen. In other words, at least in some asthma sufferers, asthmatic attacks can be triggered by learned cues. Another example is the development of frequent and chronic tension headaches. If a woman tends to get occasional tension headaches and if, when she complains of them, her chronically critical husband stops criticizing her and attends to her needs, she is obviously being reinforced for reporting the headaches. As a consequence, they are likely to increase in frequency and intensity. In this conditioning process, they are also likely to be triggered by situations in which the husband is at his most critical and/or in which the wife is particularly tired and desirous of attention.

What has the woman learned to do physically in response to these situational cues? It is likely that she has learned to make the muscles of her head, neck, and shoulders excessively tense, although she is probably unaware of doing so. Also, her overall level of muscle tension is probably higher than average. The behavior therapist would approach the treatment of this problem in exactly the same manner as we have described for previous problems. Let us examine an actual case.

Mrs. Pope, a 38-year-old housewife with four children, sought help in eliminating the tension headaches from which she had suffered practically every day for the past year. Mrs. Pope was instructed to keep careful observational records noting where and when each headache occurred and what else was happening at the time. From these notes, the therapist and patient together discovered that the headaches usually occurred upon awakening, after lunch, and in the evening after supper. Further exploration revealed that at these times Mrs. Pope was either angry at her husband for not helping with the household tasks, or she wanted to sit down and relax but felt guilty about doing so. Having thus tentatively identified the cues triggering the headaches, the therapist taught Mrs. Pope more adaptive ways of responding to these cues. Specifically, she learned to be assertive and direct in expressing her needs to her husband, and she rehearsed positive self-statements about her own worth.

The therapist also taught Mrs. Pope systematic muscle relaxation skills emphasizing the shoulders, neck, and head, and instructed her to practice for 15 minutes twice a day over a three-week period. By the end of this time, Mrs. Pope had become quite expert in judging the degree of muscle tension in these areas, and she could also detect when she began to increase the tension toward developing a headache. The therapist then taught her self-control skills; namely, she was instructed to lie down at these times whenever she could, and to attempt to relax as completely as possible for 10 to 15 minutes.

Since Mr. Pope played an active role in maintaining Mrs. Pope's headaches by being overcritical most of the time, the therapist also worked with them as a couple. Mr. Pope was helped to understand the nature of his behavior and the effect that it had on his wife. The therapist then helped Mr. and Mrs. Pope to discover ways in which Mr. Pope could give affection and attention to his wife and assisted them in initiating these new behaviors. The total treatment time required to eliminate nearly all of the headaches was three months of weekly meetings.

## Biofeedback

Biofeedback is a recently coined term which refers to any procedure in which physical behavior is continually monitored and "fed back" to the person, who is attempting to change it in any way. For example, a person who is attempting to achieve complete relaxation of the muscles of the forehead might have electrodes placed on the forehead to provide a continuous measure of muscle tension (the electromyographic or EMG response). This electrical signal would be indicated by a meter, perhaps calibrated from zero through 100. The subject would watch the meter and would try to make it go down toward zero. The meter gives immediate and continuous feedback, and also provides reinforcement for any behaviors that result in a decrease in muscle tension. Auditory rather than visual feedback can also be used. Here, the EMG signal might be converted into a tone that is high for high tension and low for low tension. The training task would be to keep the tone as low as possible and to continually try to make it go even lower. Under these conditions and with proper supervision, learning to relax specific muscle areas can be rapid and effective.

This new technology, which offers the possibility of controlling a variety of physiological responses through continuously observable feedback, has been enthusiastically embraced by psychologists and other mental health professionals as providing cures for a wide range of disorders. Unfortunately, it has also been used as the basis for exaggerated claims for the enhancement of general physical and mental well-being. Some of these claims have grown out of attempts to train persons to monitor and control their own brainwave (or electroencephalogram) patterns. Because there is a specific brain-wave pattern associated with deep relaxation and pleasant feelings, it is widely assumed that teaching people to produce this pattern in themselves has many beneficial effects. These beliefs are supported by the fact that certain Eastern mystical and religious practices involve states of consciousness that seem to be associated with similar brain-wave patterns. As yet, little or none of this work has been shown scientifically to be useful, although it is possible that EEG biofeedback might become the basis of an effective therapeutic procedure in the future.

For what purposes can biofeedback procedures validly be used? Researchers have now been able to show that excess muscle tension associated with tension headaches can be reliably reduced through biofeedback. There are also hopeful findings that biofeedback might soon be applicable to some cases of hypertension (high blood pressure) through the monitoring of one's own blood pressure. In another application, there has been much interest in treating migraine headaches by teaching patients to raise their hand temperature relative to their forehead temperature. Biofeedback equipment for this purpose involves sensitive thermometers attached to each area, and a meter that continuously displays the temperature difference. The work is based on the belief that migraine headaches are due to excessive dilation of the cranial arteries and that the temperature biofeedback procedure results in an increase in blood flow away from the head, thus decreasing dilation. As yet, however, there is no sound evidence that this procedure is effective in treating migraine headaches.

In addition to the above, exploratory studies have suggested the possibility of using biofeedback-based procedures to reduce stuttering (through the reduction of excessive muscle tension), asthma (through training in decreasing bronchial resistance to breathing), and gastric acid secretion in ulcer patients. There have also been some interesting developments in the use of biofeedback procedures in connection with physical problems that do not have an obvious psychological component, such as epilepsy, learning to reuse paralyzed muscles, and alleviating chronic pain. Clearly, there is considerable potential for the development of effective biofeedback procedures for a variety of problems. It is expected that such developments will take place once the "fad" has diminished and the current exaggerated claims of usefulness are put in perspective through sound research.

## Depression

Depression, like anxiety, is a very widespread problem among civilized people. Textbooks on psychiatry report that the majority of people seeking help for significant psychological problems show some degree of depression as part of their difficulty. As with anxiety, many perfectly well-adjusted people feel a little "low" or "blue" every now and again. Also, it is completely normal for a person to have such feelings after sustaining an important personal loss. Clinically significant depression would exist when the difficulties reach the point of interfering with the person's day-to-day functioning.

Exactly what is depression? Detailed examination of people who are called "depressed" shows that most of them share certain basic characteristics in common, although there is much variation from person to person. If this lack of precision is surprising, recall what was said in Chapter 2; namely, that the commonly used categories for problems in mental health are rather vague and unreliable and are often unhelpful in trying to determine either the origin of the difficulty or the best treatment for it.

Attempts are commonly made to identify different "types" of depression, for example, neurotic and psychotic depression, reactive and endogenous depression, and postpartum depression. It is also common to question the extent to which depression is a physically based disorder rather than a behaviorally based one. The worth of these categories and questions is somewhat doubtful. Depressive states can be brought on either by drugs or by behavior changes, and can be alleviated either by drugs or by behavioral procedures. Thus, a person's depressive difficulties could be caused by one or the other. Now that the behavioral or psychological causes are better understood, however, there is less reason for assuming a physiological cause unless it can be specifically demonstrated.

Let us list the four characteristics that depressed people tend to have in common. First, their *feelings* are primarily of sadness, pessimism, guilt, and worthlessness. Second, their *thoughts* or self-statements tend to be pessimistic, self-depreciating, and self-punishing. Third, they tend to have certain *physical complaints*, such as loss of appetite, headaches, and loss of sexual interest. Fourth, their overall *activity level* is very low, particularly in regard to pleasant activities.

Is it necessary to know how these difficulties come about in order to be able to treat them through behavior therapy? Is each set of unadaptive behaviors exhibited by a "depressed" person cued and maintained in a stable manner by events that can be identified and changed? Or is there some more basic difficulty? Experts differ on whether some people are predisposed to the development of depressive difficulties, and also on whether such a predisposition is biological or learned. Research on this question is extremely difficult to carry out. One psychologist, Martin Seligman, has conducted extensive research with animals and their responses to situations involving highly aversive but inescapable situations. He has concluded that some of the behaviors that are commonly involved in depression could indeed develop as a result of the person's perception that he cannot control his environment and that it is not worth trying to do so. This phenomenon of "learned helplessness" is one possible means by which people might become predisposed to depressive difficulties through early learning experiences.

In treating depression, behavior therapists have found it useful to focus on two separate but related aspects of the depressed person's problem: (1) difficulties in interacting with the environment; and (2) internal events—that is, the kinds of thoughts and feelings described above. Of course, depressed persons differ among themselves in the degree of difficulty in each area.

Difficulties in interacting with the environment involve the inability of depressed persons to do things that will result in positive reinforcement. They elicit few compliments, they know few ways of having fun, and many of them seldom initiate activities with others or even participate when invited to do so. In some cases this is because they do not have the necessary social or interpersonal skills. It is not difficult to understand that in order to have positive feelings about oneself, a certain amount of positive feedback from other people is needed.

Difficulties with internal events refer to the depressed person's high frequency of negative self-statements (e.g., "I am no good"), and feelings of pessimism and worthlessness. Depressed people tend to selectively focus their thoughts on the negative aspects of everyday events and to dismiss or gloss over positive aspects. Thus, difficulties which would seem minor to a normal person loom much larger to a depressed person and may seem overwhelming. Reasons for this distorted perception include unrealistically high standards that most depressed people hold for their own behavior, or think that others do, and the resulting constant self-criticism at their failure to meet these standards. In other words, they are highly self-punitive, while self-praise and self-reinforcement are very infrequent.

In treating a depressed person, the behavior therapist first attempts to identify exactly which particular unadaptive behaviors pose problems, and especially the extent to which each problem involves either environmental interaction or internal behaviors. For example, depression is the most common mental health problem among the elderly. Here almost all of the difficulties involve their interaction with the environment. Very often the stable sources of reinforcement provided by their environments disappear suddenly, as for example when a worker retires, a spouse or friends die, or a retired couple moves to Florida. Second, physical skills often tend to diminish, reducing the amount of pleasure that can be obtained from them. Important also is the fact that society's attitude toward the elderly is one of lessened value and diminished capability, and this further reduces the reinforcement available to the elderly person.

A few consistent experiences with some of the above difficulties can easily lead a person to revise downward his self-statements about his value or worth, to feel pessimistic and helpless, and to reduce his motivation for activity. This is one major way in which pessimistic and sad feelings are learned and thoughts of worthlessness developed. Another way in which these internal events can be generated is through constant repetition by a parent, spouse, or friends: "You'll never amount to anything"; or, "You never do anything right!" Once again, a person unfortunate enough to be bombarded with such statements is likely to have considerable difficulty in developing anxiety-free social skills, and might well withdraw from interaction with the environment, because "I'd never amount to anything."

Once having identified the specific problem areas, the behavior therapist addresses each in turn, and seeks to identify the cues triggering each behavior and the reinforcers maintaining it. If a lack of social skills is involved, the therapist attempts to teach these skills. In order to identify likely sources of pleasure, the patient might be asked to rate a standardized list of events and activities according to how pleasurable each is for him. In the case of losing an important source of reinforcement, such as a spouse, the therapist might encourage the patient to express grief and anger, and to explore the overall impact of this event on his life, before proceeding with specific techniques of behavior change. To change thoughts and attitudes, the therapist might negotiate with the patient to accept a slightly lower level of performance as adequate, or might instruct the patient to collect objective feedback on performance of which the patient is unduly self-critical. We have already discussed the use of teaching incompatible self-statements (e.g., "I am a worthwhile person and other people like me") in order to increase the frequency of positive thoughts and gradually diminish the effect of negative self-statements.

We have taken the view that "depression" is best regarded as a constellation of unadaptive overt and covert behaviors: pessimistic feelings, worthless thoughts, physical complaints, and motor inactivity. The emphasis on each aspect tends to differ for different people, as does the extent to which the problem involves interaction with the environment, punitive self-statements, or both. Behavior therapists find it more productive to focus on each of the specific behaviors in turn rather than to regard depression in a global manner as "neurotic" or "psychotic." We discuss depression further in Chapter 7 where work in the area of self-management is reviewed more fully.

# 5
# Interpersonal Effectiveness

In Chapter 4 we studied common psychological problems which frequently bring people to mental health professionals. In this chapter we discuss the behavioral treatment of psychological problems which are more directly interpersonal in nature. Although these problems are often not the primary reason why a person seeks professional help, they occur frequently and are often extremely distressing. We refer to difficulties such as extreme shyness, unassertiveness, difficulty in handling anger, lack of social skills, impulsive behavior, and some aspects of alcoholism.

The view that interpersonal problems are mainly a product of one's learning experiences and can be changed is rather new. The traditional belief has been that such difficulties are based on inherited traits. For example, a person with an uncontrollable temper would be thought to possess a permanent personality trait that causes the behavior. In this view, little could be done but to accept it and avoid the person during certain times. Shyness is another characteristic which has been traditionally regarded as an inborn trait. From a behavioral viewpoint, it is clear that most interpersonal difficulties involve at least the following three aspects: (a) inappropriate behavior, (b) anxiety, and (c) lack of knowledge of the appropriate interpersonal skills.

In 1962, psychologists Edward Zigler and Leslie Phillips made the important discovery that of all the psychiatric patients in a mental hospital in which they worked, those with the best social skills recovered the fastest from their difficulties and were also the least likely to be readmitted to the hospital. Conversely, those patients with the poorest social skills were the slowest to recover and were also the most likely to have difficulties in the future. The work of these psychologists has added impetus to the work of behavior therapists in developing ways of teaching interpersonal skills, with the result that a variety of effective behavioral procedures now exist. Since interpersonal problems tend to involve a specific lack of information or interpersonal skill, such as dating or conversation, a major part of the therapeutic procedure involves structured repetitive practice of new behaviors, with feedback and reinforcement.

## Assertiveness

One area of behavior therapy that has been particularly successful in capturing the popular interest is training in assertive behavior. There are a number of possible reasons for the popularity of this area, including the recent increase in respect for individual human rights of all persons and groups, and society's increasing tolerance of a wide range of acceptable behaviors, lifestyles, and general preferences.

What is assertive behavior? Early behavior therapists tended to use this term for teaching passive people to stand up for their rights, to say things that might make others angry, and to express their own anger appropriately. More recently, the notion of assertive behavior has been broadened to include the ability to forthrightly express and receive positive statements, such as compliments and an accurate evaluation of one's own worth. Thus, assertiveness is now usually defined as the ability to be direct in expressing one's beliefs and feelings in a way that also respects the rights of the other person.

Psychologists Arthur Lange and Patricia Jakubowski have presented a comprehensive approach to assertiveness training in their recent book *Responsible Assertive Behavior*. First, the person must learn the difference between assertive behavior and aggressive behavior on the one hand, and nonassertive behavior on the other. Second, the person is helped to identify and accept his own personal rights and also the rights of others. The third step is to reduce existing obstacles to assertive behavior, such as excessive anxiety, guilt, and anger, or irrational thoughts. The person is thus prepared for the fourth and final step of actually developing new assertive behaviors through direct practice. We now examine each of these steps in detail.

**Discriminating assertive behavior.** First let us contrast assertive behavior with aggressive behavior and with nonassertive behavior. As an example, consider the situation where somebody you do not know very well has asked to borrow your car. An aggressive response might be: "What! Borrow my car! You must be nuts!" A nonassertive response might be: "Well, let's see . . well, uh, the brakes aren't very good. And . . uh, I think I might have a flat tire." Contrast these with an assertive response: "No, I'm sorry, I wouldn't feel comfortable lending you my car." The assertive response gives the message directly and forthrightly, while not embarrassing the other person. The nonassertive response, by contrast, gives the impression that the person has no right to refuse, and is delivered in a self-effacing manner. The aggressive response is certainly straightforward, but it violates the personal rights of the other person by humiliating him and denying his right to make the request.

The behavior therapist might use either of two procedures in helping a client to discriminate between assertive, aggressive, and nonassertive statements. One is similar to procedures which we have discussed many times previously. The client is asked to keep daily notes of situations in which the question of assertiveness has arisen. Each situation is discussed with the therapist in turn, in order to identify the different kinds of responses that could have been made. The other procedure involves the use of structured training exercises. For example, the client might see a short film or hear a tape recording of an interpersonal situation in which a particular response has been made. Discussion then addresses the question of whether or not the response was appropriately assertive for the situation. Structured exercises are particularly useful in assertiveness training in groups, and can serve as a way of initiating a discussion among the members and prompting them to make assertive statements of their own.

**Understanding people's rights.** The second step in assertiveness training has to do with understanding and accepting people's rights, both yours and the other person's. In our society, everybody has the right to express his own feelings, thoughts, and beliefs in any way that does not violate other people's right to do the same. Nonassertive people tend to believe that they do not have this right, and in order to be able to act assertively, they must first understand clearly that they do indeed have the right to do so. Aggressive people have no difficulty in accepting their right to express their own feelings, thoughts, and beliefs, but they do so in a manner that does not take into consideration the feelings, thoughts, and beliefs of other people. This attitude is communicated both verbally and nonverbally through manner of speech, tone of voice, and abruptness. It is important to understand that aggressive people are often just as uncomfortable with assertion as are nonassertive people but handle their discomfort differently. It is not uncommon for people with difficulty in assertion to respond to one set of cues or type of situation with nonassertive behavior and to another set of cues with aggressive behavior.

Training people to identify and accept their "human rights" involves two steps. First, each person must identify personal rights that are legitimate but not accepted by the person, making it difficult to be appropriately assertive. For example, the members of an assertiveness training group might be asked to prepare a list of human rights. Each person then selects one right which he would like to have but does not feel entitled to. Group discussion then provides reassurance that this is indeed a legitimate right for any person to have. The second step involves exploration of the consequences of accepting and acting on particular rights. This exploration, which can be done either in imagery or in a role-playing situation, deals with the way in which life would be different if the person acted on a right. Included would be rehearsal of possible new behaviors, anticipation of other people's responses, and clarification of new thoughts and feelings.

**Identifying obstacles.** As a person begins to explore the possibility of accepting new rights and understanding how this would result in further changes in his life, he identifies obstacles that are currently preventing him from being comfortable with assertive behavior. These obstacles are usually thoughts ("I'll never be able to do it" or "What if he gets angry at me?") or feelings, most commonly anxiety. Here, it is often helpful for persons who are learning assertive behaviors to recognize how their unadaptive behaviors (either nonassertive or aggressive) were originally taught to them by the family and culture in which they grew up. The behavior therapist is now in a position to employ standard procedures for assisting the person to overcome these obstacles. For example, anxiety can be reduced through desensitization.

**Rehearsing new behaviors.** In the fourth and final step, the client picks specific life situations in which he would like to be more assertive and develops appropriately assertive behaviors for these actual situations. For example, a man who wants to tell his boss that he is constantly being required to do an unrealistic amount of work would utilize the therapist's help in formulating appropriate ways to make this statement to the boss. The actual words to be used would then be rehearsed in a role-playing situation with the therapist or in imagery, and the client would also formulate ways of coping with various responses that the boss might make. When the client is confident of his ability to verbalize his exact needs he would be asked to arrange the situation in real life and to actually go through with it. In the vast majority of cases where the person has rehearsed well, the outcome is more favorable than anticipated. Appropriately assertive behavior opens up a situation for frank discussion, and because it involves recognition and respect for the other person's rights, it is not as threatening to the other person as the client anticipates. Thus, the catastrophic consequences that people often fear rarely occur.

## Case Example

Let us now study the case of Mr. Thomas, a 24-year-old married man who sought help to overcome his extreme passivity and his difficulty in beginning work on his master's thesis. In the initial interview, Mr. Thomas readily agreed that he had developed a completely unassertive life-style in which his goal was to be as unobtrusive as possible. He smiled constantly and continually made jokes, most of them belittling himself. Although he was six feet tall, Mr. Thomas had the constant feeling that he was smaller and physically weaker than other people. It also became apparent during the initial interview that his master's thesis would involve a considerable amount of assertion, since it would involve organizing and producing a radio program. He expressed the desire to improve his general assertiveness before tackling this project.

The therapist began by helping Mr. Thomas to discriminate assertive behavior from aggressive behavior and from nonassertive behavior. Mr. Thomas was already skilled in perceiving nonassertive behavior, which included practically everything he did. However, he was not able to perceive the difference between aggressive behavior and assertive behavior. The therapist had him identify situations in his life in which assertive behavior was required, and asked him to describe what this behavior should be. Mr. Thomas felt that, in order to be effective, the assertive behavior would have to contain so much force as to be irresistible. For example, Mr. Thomas owned a picture that was hanging in an office now occupied by somebody else. The therapist asked him how an assertive person might go about getting it back. Mr. Thomas experienced great difficulty with this question, and finally said: "What should I do? March in there and tell them they have to give me the picture or I'll blow their brains out? What if they say 'No'?" The therapist responded by labeling this response as aggressive, and modeling what would be normally assertive behavior in the situation; namely, to announce that the picture belonged to him and that he had come to collect it.

Another situation involved a visit to his wife's parents, who would ask him what he had been doing lately. His usual response was to mumble something about doing nothing in particular but to wish that he could tell them to go to hell and that it was none of their business. Once again, Mr. Thomas and the therapist worked out an appropriately assertive response, which involved making a brief prepared statement of what he had actually been doing and then asking them in turn what they had been doing. Mr. Thomas and the therapist discussed several other situations in the same manner, labeling Mr. Thomas' inappropriate responses as aggressive or nonassertive and working out alternative assertive responses.

The second step in assertion training for Mr. Thomas was to convince him that he, like everybody else, had human rights. During discussion on this topic, Mr. Thomas revealed that he believed himself obligated to support his parents financially as soon as he had completed his master's degree. He believed he did not have the right to refuse, even though neither his sister nor his brother planned to contribute to parental support, nor did his parents appear to need support. It was Mr. Thomas' belief that he did not have the right to question his parents about this, just as he felt that he did not have the right to question anybody older than himself or in a position of higher status. Also, he believed that everything he did must be correct and that he did not have the right to make mistakes. A further belief was that he did not have the right to express his views and opinions to anybody in an authoritative position, such as his in-laws or his academic advisor.

As Mr. Thomas began to question whether he should change these beliefs and accept the personal rights which he was denying himself, a number of obstacles preventing appropriate assertive behavior now became readily apparent. For example, he expressed the strong fear that he would be physically struck by any person to whom he asserted himself. He also felt extremely guilty because he perceived himself as not meeting his responsibilities to his parents, his wife, and various other people. Another obstacle was his erroneous belief that people often simply did not notice him and that there was nothing effective he could do to be noticed. Because each of these problems involved a basically erroneous belief about himself, cognitive relearning procedures were used in which he and the therapist agreed on a set of self-statements that were both accurate and positive. Mr. Thomas then engaged in a systematic program of daily rehearsal of these new self-statements.

Mr. Thomas now felt comfortable enough with assertion that he requested help in beginning his master's thesis. The work involved two different situations in which he believed that considerable assertiveness would be required: negotiating a topic and a set of requirements with his advisor, and actually carrying out the requirements. Both of these situations were therefore employed in the final step of assertiveness training, namely, the development and practice of assertive behaviors in real-life situations. Mr. Thomas successfully completed his master's thesis 16 months after the beginning of therapy.

## Social Skills Training

Personal problems that involve a lack of social skills come to the attention of the behavior therapist in at least three ways. First, as discussed above, there is a direct relationship between adequacy of social skills and recovery from serious psychological disorder. Thus, many persons who have spent substantial periods of time in a psychiatric hospital are likely to lack important social skills. Second, a person might seek help specifically to develop needed social skills. Third, in working with other problems, the therapist sometimes finds that the person lacks the social skills that are needed to make further progress. This is at times true, for example, for a person with sexual difficulties, and sometimes with depressed persons.

In helping a person to develop social skills, the behavior therapist assumes the role of a direct teacher. It should be understood that persons seeking help in this area have often experienced frequent failures in their efforts at adequate social behavior, so that they usually feel defensive, helpless, and very anxious about the whole enterprise. This is particularly true for single persons in their twenties and thirties who have not been successful in forming satisfying relationships with members of the opposite sex. Thus, in addition to his role as a teacher, the therapist must design programs for anxiety reduction and for increasing the patient's motivation and frequency of positive experiences.

Today, some form of social skills training is almost always an aspect of the treatment of persons who have spent a significant amount of time in a psychiatric hospital. With the development of community mental health programs in the 1960's came a vigorous effort to help chronic or "permanent" patients in state psychiatric hospitals to develop their basic self-help and social skills to the point where they could live in more satisfying environments, either in foster homes, small group homes, or with their own families. These programs often utilize token economy procedures, which are described fully in Chapter 9. They follow the same basic learning principles and steps that are described below for structured training in social skills.

In learning social skills, the most important technical procedures are *modeling* and *structured practice*. In Western culture, most people learn their social skills during adolescence, and our society is structured in such a way as to provide adolescents with extensive modeling and supervised practice experiences in social skills. However, for the person who does not utilize these opportunities during adolescence, there are really no further "natural" opportunities to learn the skills.

An important aspect of social skills training is the giving of *information* by the therapist. This is particularly important, for example, in teaching dating skills to persons who did not learn them during the course of adolescence. Knowing what to say during a phone call to a member of the opposite sex, and when to make such a call, or how to make and recognize "passes" indicative of possible sexual interest, and how to handle a rejection, all involve a substantial quantity of information. Another area in which patients often need information in order to develop satisfactory skills is in learning to achieve sexual satisfaction.

We now study two case examples involving the teaching of social skills. One involves a shy and highly anxious college student who wished to learn dating skills, and the other involves a formerly homosexual man who had made the deliberate decision to become heterosexual, and who wished to learn normal masculine behaviors, including skills in interacting with women.

### Case Example: Dating and Social Skills

Ken, a 20-year-old college male, came to the therapist with the specific request to learn to date and interact socially with girls. He had very high anxiety in this area and confessed to the therapist that he had never had a date. Several years ago he had been admitted to a psychiatric hospital, where his diagnosis had been paranoid schizophrenia. His current request for therapy was a rather specific one: to be able to date girls whom he met in his classes at the university and to interact with them in a comfortable manner.

The therapist first set out to reduce his extremely high interpersonal anxiety through systematic desensitization in imagery, using a hierarchy of items developed together by Ken and the therapist. Some sample items are as follows.

1. Seeing on the street a girl who is in one of my classes.
2. Deliberately sitting near a particular girl.
3. Asking a girl to borrow her class notes.
4. Asking a particular girl for a coffee date after class.
5. Walking back to the dormitory with a girl after a date.

When Ken had been desensitized to most of the 30 items in the hierarchy, the therapist assigned him to carry out one or two of the least anxiety-producing items in real life. However, Ken failed to do so, and it became clear that he would need much more preparation.

The therapist decided to utilize direct behavior rehearsal and enlisted the help of a young married female graduate student in psychology. The intention was to have Ken rehearse with her simple conversations and requests for dates. However, simply sitting in the same room with her made Ken so anxious that it required the remainder of the session (40 minutes) to calm him down. At the next session, therefore, the therapist sat in the room with Ken and an empty chair, in which Ken was to *imagine* that a girl was sitting. Ken and the therapist then formulated and rehearsed various ways of asking for a coffee date and also formulated and rehearsed a wide variety of responses that a girl might make. Different ways in which Ken could reply to these responses were also formulated and rehearsed. Ken then turned toward the empty chair and rehearsed asking for a date, with the therapist filling in the responses. This formulation and rehearsal took two one-hour sessions.

The female graduate student now returned, and this time Ken was able to engage in extensive behavior rehearsal with her. At the end of the session, he said that he was ready to do the same thing in real life. In order to keep his feelings of anxiety to a manageable level, he agreed with the therapist's suggestion that he start with a girl who was not highly attractive to him.

At the next therapy session Ken reported that he had asked the most attractive girl in his largest class for a coffee date, and that she had accepted. Further, he had told a married friend, who had invited them both to dinner if she would be willing to come. The coffee date had gone well, and the girl had accepted the dinner invitation! Ken was in a state of high excitement and high anxiety. The therapist scheduled two additional meetings with him before the dinner date, and used this time for information and rehearsal regarding normal social etiquette. Included were meeting the girl at her dormitory, ushering her in and out of the car, introducing her to the host and hostess, initiating and maintaining conversation, and returning her to the dormitory. Ken was also encouraged to limit his expectations about the extent of the relationship that she would be willing to have with him.

The following session Ken appeared very pleased with himself, and reported that the dinner date had gone very well. The most difficult aspect of the evening had occurred when he had gone to the dormitory to pick her up, and found her holding hands with another boy who was just leaving her from a previous date. Ken had not allowed this to disturb him, however, and said that he now felt confident in his ability to date other girls.

### Case Example: Social and Masculine Behaviors

Mr. Reed, a 24-year-old formerly homosexual man, was referred by another psychologist with whom he had worked on the question of whether to seek a heterosexual adjustment. Having made a decision to become exclusively heterosexual, he now wished to learn a variety of new behaviors in that area. Much of the behavior therapist's work with this man involved direct reorientation of sexual behaviors, utilizing the procedures described in Chapter 6. Of interest in the present chapter is the work on his social behavior. This work involved two areas: (1) learning social and dating behaviors with women, and (2) learning to replace a number of effeminate motor behaviors with normal masculine behaviors. Although some of these difficulties are similar to those of Ken, Mr. Reed's goals for treatment were much more ambitious, and the treatment procedures were therefore somewhat different.

We first describe how Mr. Reed learned social skills with women. As in the previous case, Mr. Reed possessed a high degree of social anxiety which had so far prevented him from learning the desired behaviors. Treatment involved the following tasks: observing the desired behaviors modeled by others, formulating appropriate introductory statements and conversation topics, imaginal systematic desensitization to reduce high anxiety, live behavior rehearsal with the therapist and also rehearsal in imagery, and step-by-step practice in real life in which successive approximations to the desired behavior were attempted and reinforced.

There were two avenues from which women were potentially available to Mr. Reed. First, the therapist asked Mr. Reed to make a list of all the women he knew, even slightly, who would possibly be available for social interaction or dating. With some encouragement, Mr. Reed came up with a list of six women. The second avenue was a singles lounge which he had occasionally visited with his (male) cousin. However, Mr. Reed would simply sit uncomfortably and escape as soon as possible. Interestingly, he believed that the way in which a man normally initiated a conversation with a woman was to ask her to engage in sexual intercourse.

In order to teach conversational skills, the therapist and Mr. Reed together prepared a list of topics on which Mr. Reed could converse for a short time. These topics included the music being played in the lounge, how frequently each of them visited the lounge, current political issues in the nearby major city, the woman's occupation, and what each of them liked about the town. The therapist taught Mr. Reed how to introduce a topic directly, how to ask open-ended questions which would encourage further conversation from the woman, how to reinforce her further conversation, and how to make further conversation himself.

The therapist and Mr. Reed spent three sessions rehearsing these conversational skills. Initially, the therapist modeled both sides of a conversation, and then Mr. Reed took his own role. During these sessions, a lengthy hierarchy of social situations was also developed, and systematic desensitization in imagery was begun in order to reduce Mr. Reed's anxiety about them. Since some of these imaginal situations involved initiating and developing a conversation, the conversational skills were rehearsed in imagery as well as in role playing with the therapist.

As a next step, Mr. Reed agreed to make two trips to the singles lounge in order to observe the behavior of other men in initiating contacts with women. He was to go immediately to the bar, buy himself a drink, and then sit there without making any attempt to interact. Instead, he was to observe closely any single man who came through the door, in order to see how he went about initiating a contact with a woman, and what the outcome was.

At the next therapy session Mr. Reed reported that to his surprise, most of the men seemed to have some difficulty in establishing contact with a woman. He had formerly believed that he was the only man who had difficulty in this area, and that all other men initiated immediate and satisfying contacts by doing little more than snapping their fingers. Mr. Reed agreed to accept the homework assignment of initiating conversations with two different women at the singles lounge during the following week. The therapist emphasized that each conversation need not last more than a few minutes and that he was not to expect to develop a lasting relationship. Rather, he was to regard the evening as completely successful when he had completed his assignment, and he was to leave by himself.

The therapist and Mr. Reed once again rehearsed the usual introductory openings, such as a request to dance, permission to sit down, or an offer to buy the woman a drink. Mr. Reed was able to carry out the assignment successfully, and he was surprised to discover that the women with whom he spoke seemed nervous and that they also appeared to like him. During these weeks, Mr. Reed had also been able to practice his conversation skills with three of the women on his list: one at his place of employment, one in a supermarket, and one at the home of a friend.

The therapist believed that Mr. Reed was now ready for a simple dating situation. Together they identified three movie theaters in or near Mr. Reed's town, and he agreed to ask one of two women on this list for a movie date. The therapist emphasized that this was to be a practice situation for him, and that he was not to seek or expect a highly positive response from the woman. They also rehearsed a number of specific social behaviors: what to say when talking on the phone, how to request a date, how to accept a refusal, and how to arrange to call for the woman. Particularly emphasized was bidding her good night without expecting extensive physical contact, and helping Mr. Reed to understand that kissing and petting should develop out of shared interpersonal comfort rather than a sense of pressure.

Mr. Reed carried out the assignment successfully, and the following week he arranged a similar date with a woman whom he had met at the singles lounge. Over the next few weeks he was able to further expand his social contacts, and he now began to question some of his previously held attitudes about being unattractive to women and having nothing to say.

The therapist focused next on the task of helping Mr. Reed learn to substitute normal masculine behaviors for a variety of effeminate behaviors. The behaviors which he particularly wanted to change were the high pitch and intonation of his voice, the way he wiggled his hips when he walked, the way he sat, and his effeminate hand and arm movements.

To help Mr. Reed change his voice pitch and intonation, the therapist tape-recorded Mr. Reed's speech and had him study it and identify specific examples of the aspects that he wished to change. He found that he could readily lower his pitch simply by paying attention to it. After a little practice, he was also able to change his undesired intonation, which consisted mainly of becoming softer and sometimes inaudible at the end of a sentence. Mr. Reed had a tape recorder at home, and since he found that he could readily make the desired changes, he was highly motivated to practice.

Mr. Reed was much less certain about his ability to change the way he walked, as he had tried unsuccessfully to do so several times before. In order to expose him to appropriate models, the therapist instructed him to walk down the main street of his town during a busy time when the sidewalk was quite crowded. He was to select a man who was walking somewhat in front of him, and copy exactly the way he walked—his length of stride, his pace, and his arm and hand movements. Mr. Reed agreed to select at least one model each day and to spend 10 to 15 minutes in this activity.

The following week he reported that his new way of walking felt rather strange at first, but that he was becoming accustomed to it. The biggest change involved a considerable increase in the length of his stride and a secondary change was an increase in the degree to which he swung his arms. When he made these two changes, the hip wiggling disappeared automatically. He was pleased with this discovery but was rather embarrassed to use his new walk because he felt that people would notice how different it was and laugh at him. The therapist reassured him that it was exactly like other men and suggested that he practice it initially where he was not likely to meet anyone that he knew.

The therapist next had Mr. Reed engage in further modeling to learn how men and women walked together. He did this by sitting on a bench in a large shopping mall and watching how a man walked with a woman, paying attention to details of pace, conversation, and physical contact. He then closed his eyes and imagined that he was in fact that man engaging in exactly the same behavior. He engaged in this procedure once or twice a week over a four-week period and was able to transfer some of his new learning into his own social interactions with women. At the end of the treatment program, Mr. Reed had not fully achieved his goals but had made more changes than he had believed possible, and possessed sufficient self-management skills to continue his new learning on his own.

## Impulsive Acting-Out

A number of other interpersonal problems could be appropriately discussed in this chapter. One of the most distressing is impulsive acting-out, in which a person suddenly engages in unexpected and distressing activity, usually involving physical violence against people or property. This behavior can occur in public, leading to possible arrest or the loss of one's job, or in private domestic situations as an aspect of marital and family conflicts.

Persons who engage in impulsive acting-out typically report that the experience is one of two kinds. In one kind of experience, the person tends either to "go blank" and to regain awareness only after the incident has occurred, or to retain awareness in the sense of being a spectator or a passive observer of the behavior, which almost seems to belong to somebody else. In the other kind of experience, the person is acutely aware of the danger of acting out and struggles for control before giving in to the impulse.

Impulsive acting-out can involve a number of different behaviors and motivations, including anger and physical violence, sexual deviations, and drug abuse. In the present context we emphasize acting-out that involves anger. Although losing one's temper rather obviously involves the expression of anger, it is interesting that some persons with a chronic problem of acting out with physical violence do not perceive anger to be an important problem. However, such people almost always lack the skills to express their dissatisfaction, irritation, or annoyance in an appropriate way, and they also tend to lack normal assertive skills to ensure their rights.

The term "impulsive" usually means "without thinking." In other words, behavior that is labeled impulsive usually occurs without the thoughts, or self-statements, that for most people accompany the experience of angry feelings. Most people acknowledge the experience of angry feelings, at least to themselves, with a thought such as: "This is beginning to make me angry; how should I handle it?" An impulsive person, however, might act automatically in response to the feelings without engaging in such thoughts at all. In fact, some people barely even recognize the existence of angry feelings, but respond directly with action to cues that would normally trigger such feelings, and then are genuinely surprised to find that they have been shouting or have punched the other fellow.

In treating a problem of impulsive anger, the main task is to teach the person to make appropriate verbal statements rather than acting out. The behavior therapist has the person keep a daily record of every situation in which he experiences any angry feelings at all, together with notes on the nature of the situation and the outcome. Since the task is to learn to engage in appropriate thoughts as soon as the angry feelings are perceived, the therapist has the patient rehearse appropriate self-statements, such as "This is making me angry" or "I feel like hitting him." The therapist and patient then rehearse together some of these situations, and the patient says aloud the appropriate self-statements that will ultimately become covert.

The next step is to predict what anger-arousing situations are likely to occur in the patient's coming week and to rehearse appropriate ways of responding. This can be done both covertly in imagery and also overtly in role-playing, stating the angry feelings whenever it is appropriate to do so. The patient is once again instructed to keep daily records. It is usual to find that initially, the patient's frequency of reported angry feelings increases dramatically, and the patient's thoughts about being angry also increase dramatically. One patient, a 28-year-old man who had the problem of impulsively hitting somebody approximately once a week, stated that after a week of record-keeping he became "practically obsessed" with angry thoughts and feelings. Rather than hitting people, however, he spent a great deal of time telling his family and workmates how angry he was. In doing so, he learned that it was perfectly acceptable to feel angry and to talk about it. He also was able to identify what he was angry about; or, in behavioral language, he identified the cues triggering his angry thoughts and feelings.

# Alcoholism

This chapter would not be complete without a brief description of the behavioral view of the nature and treatment of alcoholism. As described in Chapter 2, aversive or punishment procedures for the treatment of alcoholism were in use as long as 30 years ago, but with rather limited success. It is only in the last few years that behavior therapists have clearly understood the necessity for teaching excessive drinkers adaptive ways of responding to the difficulties that currently trigger their drinking behavior and that it is not sufficient simply to punish the person's drinking behavior.

Behavioral scientists studying the treatment of alcoholism have made another recent discovery, which has met with considerable resistance from many professionals in this area. We are referring to the finding that many problem drinkers can be successfully trained to engage only in "social drinking." Theorists who regard alcoholism as a "disease" believe that the only possible goal is total abstinence. From a behavioral viewpoint, however, it is possible that the cues controlling social drinking behavior might be quite different from the cues controlling excessive drinking. Even when the two sets of cues are rather similar, it should be possible to teach the patient to carefully discriminate between them, and thus to learn that social situations provide cues for social but not excessive drinking. Thus, the critical task for the behavior therapist and the patient is to determine the exact cues that trigger *excessive* drinking behavior. Excessive drinking behavior is strengthened, of course, by the negative reinforcement of immediate anxiety reduction, which has a much more powerful influence on the person's behavior than the long-range aversive consequences. This is a way of explaining the "addictive" effect of alcohol, which refers to the fact that taking a drink has the *immediate* positive reinforcing effect of making the person feel better but the *long-range* aversive effect of increasing the difficulties. Because immediate contingencies, even small ones, tend to be more effective than delayed contingencies, even powerful ones, drinking will continue even though it makes the person's overall problem worse.

Once the cues have been identified, the next step is to teach the person alternative ways of responding to them. Often the cues involve interpersonal stress, particularly social anxiety or fear of failure in a job. In deciding whether or not social drinking would be a feasible therapeutic goal for a patient, the therapist would examine situations in which social drinking would occur to determine whether they contain the cues that trigger excessive drinking.

People who have at least one parent who is an excessive drinker are more likely than average to become excessive drinkers as adults. Behavioral psychologists believe that such a parent serves as a model in teaching this unadaptive behavior. Also, alcoholics are more likely than average to have spouses who also drink excessively. As stated above, drinking has an immediate and obvious anxiety-reduction effect; for this and other reasons, it can serve as a convenient escape from life's stresses. Unfortunately, such escape behavior through anxiety reduction is reinforced and can thus become habitual. Whether or not this is the major way in which problem drinking behavior is maintained, it is certainly an important aspect for many alcoholics.

Excessive drinkers are difficult to work with in therapy because of certain characteristics which they tend to have in common. First, they consistently tend to deny the full extent of their alcohol intake, so that their daily record of drinking is often grossly inaccurate. In other words, they are poor self-observers and reporters. Second, they tend to make self-statements at a high rate excusing their drinking as acceptable behavior, or "rationalizing" it. Third, they are often unwilling to subject themselves to the necessary discipline required in a therapeutic program that involves a significant amount of personal effort. This is perhaps another way of stating the traditional belief that most alcoholics must go all the way down before they can come up again.

The behavioral treatment of problem drinking involves three basic steps, the extent of each depending on the particular patient. First, as with any other problem behavior, it is necessary to help the patient change or manage those problem situations in his environment that generally appear to be associated with drinking, such as an intolerable marriage or chronic pressure at work. The therapist uses procedures such as assertiveness training and systematic desensitization, and also works directly with other members of the patient's environment either to change unadaptive behaviors or to train them as change agents. It might also be necessary to teach the patient social skills that are currently lacking.

The second step, an extension of the first, is to have the patient keep systematic drinking records in order to determine the exact nature of the cues triggering drinking, and then plan to remove them or systematically teach new responses to them. The third step, not always required, is a systematic course of aversive conditioning to alcoholic beverages and to "high-risk" situations. Recent research has reported some degree of success using mild electric shock conditioning for this purpose; a more flexible conditioning procedure involves aversive imagery, also called covert sensitization. Both of these procedures have their effect through teaching the person to become anxious in the presence of the cues that he is trying to avoid. Aversive imagery procedures are discussed fully in Chapter 6 in the context of describing the treatment of deviant sexual behavior such as exhibitionism.

# 6

# Sexual and Marital Problems

The treatment of sexual and marital problems has been an area of rapid progress in the past 10 to 15 years. Several related factors have contributed to this progress. One is society's increasing willingness to accept as normal an increasingly wider range of personal and interpersonal behaviors. Another has been the pioneering research efforts in the scientific study of sexual behaviors, both normal and abnormal. A third is the development of behavioral treatment technology, which has provided the necessary tools for the successful design of procedures to change unwanted and distressing sexual behaviors and attitudes. In general, people are nowadays more willing to acknowledge their sexual problems and to seek help, courts are more willing to prescribe and collaborate with treatment programs for sexually deviant persons, society is more willing to view homosexuality as within the normal range of sexual preferences, and the seeking of professional assistance in dealing with marital difficulties is now commonplace.

## Common Sexual Difficulties

### The Work of Masters and Johnson

The past 10 to 15 years have brought about a truly major revolution in the understanding and treatment of common sexual difficulties. This is due in large part to the courageous and painstaking research of William H. Masters and Virginia Johnson. Masters and Johnson published their first book, *Human Sexual Response*, in 1966, and followed it in 1970 with a detailed report of their treatment program, *Human Sexual Inadequacy*. It is ironic that while their concepts and methods are directly behavioral in nature, no direct reference to behavior therapy is made in either volume, nor do Masters or Johnson identify themselves in any way as behavior therapists.

Because the work of Masters and Johnson is mainly behavioral, it has been enthusiastically embraced and extended by behavior therapists. The procedures described in this chapter can thus be seen as both in the mainstream of current behavior therapy and as a direct development from the original Masters and Johnson procedures as described in their 1970 volume.

As adapted by behavior therapists, treatment procedures for sexual dysfunction are nowadays more flexible and probably even more effective than the original Masters and Johnson work. Behavior therapists have been able to refine and extend the original work by viewing it as the application of concepts such as modeling, shaping, reinforcement, and desensitization. In addition, a number of conditions that Masters and Johnson believed to be essential for therapeutic success have been shown to be unnecessary, except perhaps in a few cases. For example, it is not necessary, as Masters and Johnson believed it was, to work intensively within a concentrated period of time (for example, two weeks full-time) away from the couples' home. Rather, therapy can be conducted successfully using once-weekly sessions, as with the treatment of many other problems.

Since sexual responses are to a high degree under the control of specific stimuli, and since the major ongoing stimulus for these responses is a person's sexual partner, it is usually considered essential to have the partner present and available at all times. In fact, one of the major contributions made by Masters and Johnson was to point out that treatment must involve both partners as a fully cooperating unit. More recently, there have been reports of treatment of sexual problems in which only one person was involved in therapy; such cases, however, are the exception to the rule.

In comparing the era before Masters and Johnson with today's procedures for treating sexual difficulties, two major differences are apparent. The first has to do with the way in which sexual problems were formerly viewed theoretically by mental health professionals. The prevailing viewpoint was the one originally put forward by Sigmund Freud, in which such difficulties as impotence and orgasmic dysfunction (frigidity) were thought to be surface effects of deep-seated psychological disorders having their origins in early childhood. Treatment involved extensive dynamically oriented psychotherapy, aimed at developing insight into the basic psychological disorder and thereby resolving it. The sexual difficulty itself was largely ignored in this process but was expected to disappear once the presumed basic conflicts were resolved. Not surprisingly, therapeutic success was quite limited.

In contrast to this traditional approach, Masters and Johnson viewed sexual difficulties either as an outcome of specific inappropriate learning experiences, a simple lack of information or knowledge of sexual skills, faulty attitudes regarding sexuality, or, more commonly, a combination of these factors. Thus, their treatment procedures included the provision of basic information, the modification of attitudes, and the learning or relearning of normal sexual behaviors.

The second major difference today as compared with the era before Masters and Johnson reflects the degree to which these researchers were instrumental in removing the stigma associated with sexual difficulties and with public discussion of normal sexuality. The original work in combating society's closed attitudes toward sexuality was done by research scientist Alfred Kinsey and his co-workers in the late 1940's. Kinsey's work began a gradual change in public attitudes toward sexuality as a legitimate topic for scientific investigation and a move away from the Victorian view of sexuality as shameful, obscene, and immoral. Building on Kinsey's groundwork, Masters and Johnson were able to develop the scientific basis for current therapeutic approaches to sexual difficulties, showing that they are best viewed within the context of faulty or inadequate learning. By themselves modeling attitudes of openness, scientific legitimacy, and an absence of shame or embarrassment, Masters and Johnson have contributed heavily to the development of changed attitudes in most mental health professionals and in an increasingly large sector of society.

## Impotence and Orgasmic Dysfunction

The two common sexual difficulties that are perhaps the most widely known are *impotence* in the male, or consistent inability to achieve and maintain an erection that is sufficient to penetrate the vagina, and frigidity or *orgasmic dysfunction* in the female, the inability to reach orgasm during sexual intercourse. From the extensive research conducted by Masters and Johnson on the physiology of the human sexual response, we know that the immediate cause of both of these disorders is a failure of the basic physiological response involved in sexual arousal, namely, *vasocongestion*, an increase in blood supply to the genital organs. Masters and Johnson showed that both males and females with these disorders tended to share common backgrounds and beliefs: sexual inexperience, false information, and unresolved conflicts regarding sexual taboos. For males, there is high anxiety about sexual performance; for females, usually a background involving strict traditional religious values and teaching of strongly negative values about sexuality. Thus, a common link among persons with such difficulties is a high degree of anxiety, either about their ability to perform normal sexual behaviors or about the propriety of doing so. As far as researchers understand, this anxiety plays a basic and major part in preventing vasocongestion and thus normal sexual responding. It also leads such people to avoid sexual contact.

Nowhere is the behavioral treatment principle of small repetitive structured steps more important than in the treatment of sexual dysfunction. In the original procedures of Masters and Johnson and also in the refinement of these procedures by behavior therapists, small structured steps are utilized as a vehicle for two major behavioral treatment techniques: (a) desensitization of anxiety; and

(b) modeling, rehearsal, and shaping of new behaviors. Treatment for impotence and for orgasmic dysfunction involves a detailed hierarchy of behaviors to be performed together by the couple over the course of treatment. Usually the therapist explicitly instructs the couple to refrain from any sexual behaviors other than those prescribed. Most important, it must be clearly understood that there is to be no attempt at intercourse until that particular behavior is reached in the therapeutic hierarchy.

The first behavior in the hierarchy, performed over a period of days, is generally simple touching and caressing of each other's naked bodies in comfortable, relaxed privacy. The partners take turns touching and caressing each other in ways that produce no anxiety, and any contact with the sexual organs or female breasts is absolutely forbidden. This exercise serves to desensitize the couple to anxiety associated with the presence of each other's nakedness and touch. Also, it gives them the opportunity to experience sensual pleasure in the absence of explicit sexual behavior. Specific aids for increasing pleasure can include deep muscle relaxation, gentle massage, and the use of oils and lotions to provide a smooth soft touch and enhance sensuality. These exercises have variously been called "pleasuring" and "sensate focus."

When both partners have become comfortable and free from anxiety at the first step in the hierarchy, the therapist instructs them to progress to the next step. This involves an increase in the scope of the pleasurable caressing to include brief movements near to, and perhaps brushing over, the erogenous areas of the body, including the pelvic areas and the breasts in the female. Once again, progress should be slow enough that little or no anxiety is aroused. Each partner is instructed to give feedback to the other in order to avoid anxiety-producing behaviors, and also, to identify what kinds of touching and caressing are the most pleasurable. The second step serves to further desensitize the couple to anxiety over nakedness, intimacy, and being caressed, and also serves to develop skills in the giving of sensual pleasure to the partner. The third step in the hierarchy involves active caressing of the genital areas. Here, each partner in turn gives the other ongoing instruction and feedback as to what specific movements create the greatest pleasure. Once again, there is no demand for erection in the male or arousal in the female, although by the time this step of the hierarchy has been reached, definite arousal usually occurs.

**Impotence.** From this point, the treatment of impotence progresses as follows. In the next item in the desensitization and instructional hierarchy, the couple continues mutual pleasuring and caressing, but with the women kneeling alongside his body and facing him. In the next step, she straddles his body in a position from which she can easily insert the penis in her vagina if it should be erect and if the man is comfortable with it. Further steps include gentle movements by the woman to the man's instruction, and further progression at a pace which keeps the man's anxiety minimal or absent, so that his confidence at achieving an erection eventually reaches a sustained level.

As in working with other problems where new types of skills are to be learned, active instruction is a very important part of the therapeutic procedure for sexual dysfunction. The use of films which model normal sexual functioning have been found to be extremely useful, both for their arousal value and for their modeling of attitudes and actual behaviors. It is also important to understand that the therapeutic process involves much more than simple behavior change and anxiety reduction. There must be an opportunity for the expression of attitudes and beliefs and a chance to test and change them. In some cases, an opportunity is also needed to identify and discuss additional problems that appear to be connected with the sexual difficulties but which may or may not have anything to do with them. Thus, the therapist should possess sophisticated general clinical skills in addition to a sound knowledge of behavioral technology as applied to sexual dysfunction.

**Orgasmic dysfunction.** Step by step desensitization and instructional procedures have also been employed for the treatment of orgasmic dysfunction, with a promising success rate reported by Masters and Johnson for their own work. More recently, a slightly different behavioral procedure has also been employed, with perhaps higher success. In this second procedure, the ultimate response to be achieved (female orgasm) is developed first in the most rapid and convenient manner: masturbation while alone. The woman is assisted by careful prior instruction from a film or from an experienced female therapist, and often uses a vibrator. Once the desired response is achieved when alone, stepwise approximations to sexual intercourse are gradually introduced. The first of these steps could involve the man's presence in an adjacent room. When the woman is orgasmic and free from anxiety under these conditions, the next step might involve her calling her partner into the room for brief periods of time, and gradually increasing the amount of time that he spends in the room. Further steps would involve his gradual participation in the masturbation and ultimately full participation as a sexual partner.

## Other Sexual Difficulties

Several other kinds of sexual difficulties can often be successfully treated by recently developed specific techniques. The most common of these difficulties, *premature ejaculation*, is treated by the "squeeze technique," developed by urologist J. H. Semans. In this procedure the woman systematically squeezes the penis in a particular way with thumb and finger just before ejaculation is expected. Although the procedure has no obvious explanation in behavioral science, its consistent use under therapeutic supervision is reported to result in very high success rates.

*Vaginismus* is a disorder in which the vaginal muscles contract involuntarily to prevent entry of the penis. The first step in treatment is a clinical demonstration to both partners that the same contractions occur to the attempted insertion of any object (for example, medical examination instruments). This is followed by a systematic stepwise program in which the woman inserts a series of medical dilators, at first adapting to an extremely small size and then using progressively larger instruments as her comfort increases and the contractions permit.

The treatment of *ejaculatory incompetence*, a relatively uncommon difficulty in which the man can achieve a satisfactory erection but is unable to ejaculate, involves the same kind of successive approximations as the treatment of ogasmic dysfunction. Such men can ejaculate with solitary masturbation, and this step is used as a starting point for the introduction of stimuli involving progressively more and more of the elements of normal sexual intercourse.

# Homosexuality

Homosexuality is a topic on which there is now active and continuing public debate. Encouraged by increasingly flexible attitudes in society, the traditional viewpoint of homosexuality as abnormal and socially unacceptable has been actively challenged by homosexuals themselves, who have been more and more willing to identify themselves publicly in order to do so. The common belief that male homosexuals have effeminate characteristics and feminine interest patterns has been shown to be untrue for the majority of homosexuals. Although there has been extensive writing on the causes of homosexuality, little definite has been discovered. Perhaps the most consistent finding is that homosexuals have more often had pleasurable sexual experiences before adolescence and before the development of well-differentiated heterosexual behavior patterns.

Regardless of whether homosexuality should be regarded as biologically normal behavior, many persons are distressed by their homosexual thoughts, feelings, and behaviors and seek help to achieve a comfortable heterosexual adjustment. Most mental health professionals today are able to remain nonjudgmental when helping them to make the decision as to whether they wish to become heterosexual or to become more comfortable with homosexuality. Once the decision is made, behavior therapy procedures can assist the person in making either type of change.

### The Case of Mr. Thomas

In Chapter 5 we introduced Mr. Thomas, a 24-year-old man with a background of homosexual behavior who wished to become actively heterosexual, and we discussed in detail the changes which he made in the areas of social skills with women and masculine motor behavior. Let us now take an overall view of Mr. Thomas' case. Mr. Thomas was a tall, young-looking man whose movements were somewhat effeminate. He lived alone with his widowed mother, who was reportedly domineering, demanding, and controlling, treating him like a child rather than an adult. Mr. Thomas' homosexual experiences had included a number of affairs with older men, as well as a variety of casual encounters with persons of his own age. He had sporadically dated several different girls, but was always anxious and uncomfortable with them. He had attempted intercourse once with a prostitute, but had been unable to achieve an erection. Mr. Thomas reported frequent masturbation to fantasies of homosexual men.

The therapist's behavioral assessment resulted in the following six problem areas and the treatment proposed for each. First, it was planned to teach Mr. Thomas assertive skills for interacting with his mother. The second step was to involve anxiety reduction in regard to social and sexual interaction with women. Third was the teaching of specific social skills with women. Fourth, it was planned to associate sexual arousal with women. The fifth step was to eliminate sexual behaviors, thoughts, and feelings toward men. Sixth, it was planned to teach him to eliminate effeminate motor behaviors such as wiggling his hips.

The first area, teaching Mr. Thomas to be more assertive toward him mother, followed the outline for assertiveness· training as described in Chapter 5, and will not be further elaborated. The second and third areas have also been discussed in detail in Chapter 5 together with the sixth area. To work on the fourth area, the association of sexual arousal with women, the therapist had Mr. Thomas employ a masturbation procedure. The plan was to have him initiate masturbation to fantasies of males, and then switch to a female fantasy when ejaculation was imminent. However, Mr. Thomas reported experiencing no difficulty in developing an erection and completing masturbation to fantasies of females. He initially looked at centerfold pictures from Playboy magazine and later switched to fantasies of women that he knew. This aspect of treatment was completed by systematic desensitization in imagery to social interaction with these women and then making sexual requests leading to intercourse in imagery.

The fifth area involved Mr. Thomas' sexual arousal and interest in men. These were reduced through the use of aversive imagery, a procedure which is described in greater detail in the next section on deviant sexual behavior. Briefly, Mr. Thomas was trained to engage in images in which an attractive homosexual man approached him, followed immediately by aversive feelings of nausea and imaginal vomiting. In another set of aversive images, a homosexual man suddenly attacked him physically and Mr. Thomas eventually escaped only after a horrendous fight.

The therapist worked with Mr. Thomas for 23 weekly sessions, most of which were spent in teaching him social approach behaviors with women and reducing his anxiety over social and sexual contact with women. In contrast to the difficulty involved in achieving these changes, the development of changes in physical sexual responding took relatively little time. The reader should understand that this is not necessarily a typical pattern and that the range of specific difficulties associated with problems of sexual preference is extremely diverse.

## Deviant Sexual Behaviors

While there is considerable conflict in society over the degree to which homosexuality should be regarded as normal behavior, there is complete agreement that the following behaviors are completely unacceptable. We are referring to pedophelia, or *child molesting*, the use of children by adult males to gain sexual excitement, and *exhibitionism*, the public displaying of the penis, often while masturbating. Men engaging in these behaviors are subject to arrest and imprisonment, often with substantial sentences. A third disorder, also of males, is *transvestism*, in which the man gains sexual excitement from dressing as a woman, often in the company of other such men.

As with common sexual difficulties described earlier in this chapter, success in treating these disorders was low prior to the development of behavior therapy procedures. Now that behavioral treatment techniques are becoming more widely available, courts are more commonly considering treatment as an alternative to imprisonment for child molesting and exhibitionism.

What motivates a man to engage in these deviant sexual behaviors rather than in normal heterosexual behavior? A number of theories and much speculation have been offered on this topic. One plausible explanation is based on the findings that such men often have two aspects of their sexual learning history in common. First, their history often includes some form of positive reinforcement for the deviant sexual behavior in question, usually before adolescence. Second, there is often difficulty in achieving normal sexual satisfaction, due either to a lack of the needed skills, high anxiety, some other difficulty, or a combination of these factors. Curiously, these men are quite often unaware of their difficulties with normal sexual behavior, and may deny them at first when questioned. Also, they are often quite impulsive and may act rather suddenly on their urges, motivated by the prospect of immediate enjoyment without considering the further consequences of the behavior. It is not uncommon to find that a man's probability of engaging in a deviant sexual act increases after he has been drinking alcohol. The drinking, in turn, is often triggered by feelings of depression.

## Treatment Procedures

Treatment of sexually deviant behaviors follows the same strategy that is employed whenever any stable but undesired behavior is to be eliminated. First, the therapist and patient together identify the desired alternative behavior—in this case, successful sexual interactions with adult women. On occasion, a man might choose a homosexual adjustment. Second, they assess the discrepancy between the goal and what the patient is currently able to do, and then clarify the reasons for the discrepancy: lack of skills or knowledge, high interfering anxiety, or lack of opportunity. Treatment is then directed toward overcoming these deficits until the patient is able to arrange and enjoy normal sexual behavior. The final step is to reduce the attractiveness of the original problem behavior so that it is no longer the behavior of choice.

Let us follow the treatment of a 26-year-old man, Mr. Donaldson, who was referred by the courts for treatment of his child-molesting problem. The immediate event which led to his arrest involved a nine-year-old boy with whom he had been babysitting while the parents were out of town overnight. Mr. Donaldson had gotten into bed with the boy and had fondled his genitals while becoming sexually excited himself. The boy had reported the event the next day to his parents, who had pressed legal charges.

Mr. Donaldson had been arrested several times over the previous four years for similar offenses, but had either escaped the charges or had received a probationary sentence. After the therapist succeeded in impressing upon him the fact that the success of treatment would depend on his honesty about the extent of his past and present impulses toward this behavior, he described his almost daily impulses to interact sexually with boys and girls and said that he had actually carried it out on the average of once every two or three months over the past five years. As an adolescent, Mr. Donaldson had spent several years in a boys' boarding school where homosexual behavior was not uncommon.

In regard to social and sexual skills with women, Mr. Donaldson initially reported that he had had many girlfriends and was comfortable with both social interaction and sexual activity. The therapist nevertheless asked him to keep detailed notes on his behavior and feelings in interacting with his current girlfriend over a two-week period. Careful analysis of these records and further questioning showed rather clearly that Mr. Donaldson was, in fact, extremely anxious in the presence of women, and consistently did things to keep his relationships with his girlfriends on a superficial level. Exploration of his present and past relationships showed that all the efforts to maintain a relationship were made by the woman, and that although Mr. Donaldson was able to satisfactorily engage in sexual intercourse this was also initiated by the woman, who tended to play the dominant role.

**Strengthening needed behaviors.** The first step in treatment involved increasing Mr. Donaldson's conversational and social skills with women. The therapist helped him to develop a number of specific topics for conversation and to formulate some of the actual words that might be used. He was then trained in imagery skills, and desensitization was employed to a hierarchy of situations in which conversation was initiated and relationships were begun. These imaginal situations included the opportunity to use the newly formulated conversational skills. In the next step, Mr. Donaldson was required to make a list of possible locations where he might be able to meet women. This was followed by visiting several of the places and initiating conversations as rehearsed.

It should be emphasized that Mr. Donaldson's superficial social skills were excellent but were accompanied by high anxiety, and he would typically assume a dependent posture in which the woman was required to take the lead in order to maintain the interaction. Once Mr. Donaldson found that he could in fact control the relationship by being assertive and moving to take the lead, his anxiety diminished rapidly. It also became evident to Mr. Donaldson that the child molesting had been providing him with affection without any accompanying demand for a continued relationship. He discovered that women would also meet these needs if he simply told them that he did not want a continued relationship, and he was quite surprised how quickly he could now develop a high degree of comfort in his relationships with women.

**Aversive imagery.** From the beginning of treatment, Mr. Donaldson had been keeping records of the frequency of thoughts and impulses directed toward child molesting. These records showed that the thoughts or impulses occurred practically every day, with a slight reduction at the current point of treatment. In order to work toward eliminating them altogether, the therapist began an aversive imagery procedure in which Mr. Donaldson was asked to describe in detail several possible child molesting situations which could arouse a high degree of sexual excitement. He was also to select a highly aversive event that would be willing to engage in at the therapist's instruction. After discussion of alternatives, Mr. Donaldson selected feelings of nausea. It is usually possible to train persons to feel acutely nauseated by engaging them in an imaginal sequence in which they begin to feel sick to their stomachs and finally vomit, and the therapist was able to train Mr. Donaldson in this sequence quite readily. An entire therapy session was spent in aversive trials, in which Mr. Donaldson systematically imaged himself becoming excited at the prospect of molesting a child. Each time the excitement developed, the therapist directed him to vividly produce the nausea image, thereby punishing his feelings of excitement associated with child molesting.

Mr. Donaldson practiced this sequence of events daily at home for about 20 minutes. He rapidly found himself unable to utilize the same child molesting image for more than four to five consecutive trials because it became too aversive to imagine. In the next session, therefore, the therapist trained him to alternate among the number of different images. This procedure had the added advantage that he was able to cover in imagery all the situations in which child molesting might be a possibility. Mr. Donaldson continued his homework assignments with some further modifications for a total of five weeks. His daily records for the fourth and fifth weeks showed that he had had no thoughts or impulses of child molesting during that period except in the homework assignments. In addition, he reported that the homework had become so aversive and anxiety-arousing that it was extremely difficult to do. On the other hand, his social interaction with women had increased in frequency and satisfaction. A follow-up interview after six months showed that Mr. Donaldson continued to be free of child molesting, and while he did experience some infrequent thoughts about it, they were automatically followed by thoughts that it would be a foolish and anxiety-arousing activity.

**Exhibitionism and transvestism.** Essentially the same procedure is used to treat exhibitionism and transvestism. In developing an aversive procedure, a number of different variations are possible. Since all of them are (by definition) unpleasant for the patient, the therapist is careful to select a procedure that the patient is completely satisfied with and is willing to endure. In utilizing aversive imagery, other common images include the appearance of police officers, shame and ridicule, and the experience of physical punishment. Thus, the image involving a sexual exhibiting opportunity might be taken to the point where sexual excitement is first perceived by the patient, and then interrupted by the sudden appearance of two hefty policemen who arrest the patient. Another image could involve the appearance of muscular men who proceed to beat up the patient. In all of these sequences, the crucial aspect is to elicit a vivid image of the initial aspects of molesting or exhibiting, together with feelings of sexual excitement, and then to follow it as rapidly as possible with a definite aversive experience such as nausea or fear.

In the later stages of practicing these sequences, patients usually report that they can put themselves into an image involving a formerly attractive opportunity for performing the deviant behavior without experiencing any desire or impulse. When the patient has reached this point in treatment, he can be asked to test his new learning in real-life situations by putting himself in a relatively "safe" situation containing cues for the deviant behavior. The patient continues to invoke the aversive image if the slightest excitement or attraction is felt.

In the treatment of a 30-year-old transvestite, a married man with a responsible job, the most effective aversive images involved his work. In these images, the patient's boss called the patient into his office and read him a detailed detective report on his activities over the past several days. The boss then expressed his great disgust and fired him on the spot. The patient also made a tape recording in which he listed all the things he would lose if he was caught at transvestism: his wife and family, his job, and the respect of his friends and community. He played this tape 10 to 15 times a day while driving in his car. In all these procedures, of course, the criterion for success is the reduction and final disappearance of the behaviors to be eliminated and of impulses and thoughts about the behaviors.

## Marital Problems

Marital problems represent a special category of problems that arise in close interpersonal relationships. Each of us has our own history of interpersonal learning experiences in which we have been taught to value certain behaviors, beliefs, and attitudes. Such behaviors, beliefs, and attitudes are reinforcers for us. On the other hand, each of us is made anxious or angry by other behaviors, beliefs, and attitudes, which therefore represent negative reinforcers or punishment. When two or more people have an interpersonal commitment to each other, they have made an agreement to rely on the other person or persons to meet their needs (that is, to supply positive reinforcement) before looking elsewhere. Since no person's needs are a perfect match with another person's, there will always be areas in which needs are not met or in which conflict occurs. Also, people's needs change over time and with changing environments.

The term "marital problems" can have two different emphases. First, it can refer simply to the occurrence of *any* individual adjustment problem as it affects a marriage relationship. Second, it can refer to failures or conflicts in satisfying the other person's needs, as described above. Obviously, the more individual difficulties people bring to the marriage relationship, the less likely they are to be able to satisfy their partner's needs, and the more opportunities there will be for interpersonal difficulties. However, it is quite possible to have interpersonal difficulties requiring professional help between two people who would each be considered reasonably free of difficulties when taken alone.

**Sexual difficulties.** Many couples seeking professional help for marital difficulty have sexual difficulties. Conversely, many couples seeking professional help for sexual difficulties are experiencing some degree of marital conflict. More often than not, each problem interacts with and is reinforced by the other. However, couples do not always see the relevance of one to the other, and at times a couple with a specific marital conflict may even decline to answer questions about sexual matters. Since close cooperation is needed between the partners in working on specific sexual difficulties, the existence of a significant amount of marital conflict tends to interfere with the work and reduces the chances of a successful outcome.

## Gathering Assessment Data

Marital problem situations are often not what they are presented to be when initially described to the therapist. The difference between what the couple perceives to be happening and what is actually happening tends to be greater in marital difficulties than in a person's perception of his individual difficulties. Thus, while the couple is often in agreement as to the difficulties, the true situation might be different from the way they both perceive it. In other words, the couple often has some investment in maintaining the status quo, no matter how painful. If the partners differ substantially from each other in their view of the situation, by the time they seek help each has often developed a well-established rationale for his or her particular view and is eager to present it to the therapist and be proven correct.

In cases where both partners agree as to the problem, it is often agreed that one of them is primarily responsible for the difficulties. However, this person has often been bullied into accepting this view by the other. Thus, the therapist may start at a considerable disadvantage, because he may be presented with a consistent and agreed account of the difficulties that simply ignores their most important aspects. In addition, although the couple professes a desire to make changes, the two people are often extremely wary of doing so because one or both are unrealistically afraid that there might be traumatic consequences, such as breaking up the marriage. Thus, the therapist's work in discovering the real facts may be hampered by fears that the consequences of treatment will be worse than the present state of affairs. Specifically, "bullies" often believe that they will not be able to function adequately in a more normal interaction, but only in a situation where the cards are stacked in their favor. They may believe that their own needs will not be met and/or that they will not be able to meet the needs of their partner.

Because marital conflict is a difficult area in which to collect accurate behavioral observations, and because such information is necessary in order to design treatment strategies, it is advantageous to have a structured and standardized format for gathering the needed information. One such instrument is the Marital Pre-Counseling Inventory, developed by behavior therapists Richard and Frieda Stuart. This comprehensive 11-page booklet asks each of the partners to provide information on both themselves and their partner, describing actual behaviors and also ideally desired behaviors in a number of areas. Included are family composition, daily schedule, spouse behaviors that are pleasing to the other, present and future goals and plans, interests, how decisions are made, frequency of conversation on specific topics, sexual behavior, management of the children, and general satisfaction. A comparison of the inventories completed by husband and wife provides the therapist with a comprehensive data base and pinpoints areas in which more detailed questions can be asked about specific difficulties.

## Treatment Strategies

The simplest behavioral treatment in marital therapy can be employed in situations where each of the partners can readily identify specific and realistic behaviors which they would like the other to perform. The therapist acts as negotiator for them in reaching a specific agreement, so that each performs a selected behavior at agreed times during the next few days. If the negotiation is done carefully, and both partners have the freedom to select behaviors that they feel able to perform, the contract is almost always carried out. Each partner is asked to keep written notes of these situations so that communication with the therapist can be accurate. In the next session, the couple negotiate for further behaviors, and ultimately learn how to negotiate with each other without the need for a therapist.

The partners are often quite skeptical at first, and might agree to perform the new behaviors but see nothing useful that could result from it. However, their attitudes usually change after the first week, and it is not uncommon for the couple to spontaneously identify more serious problems than their first complaint and ask if they can be dealt with in the same manner. A similar type of approach can be used with partners who habitually do things which make each other very anxious or angry. Here, part of the negotiation includes an agreement *not* to do a certain thing which is aversive to the other. Each spouse should recognize that the other might have no clear understanding as to why the selected behaviors are important, nor is such an understanding necessary for a successful outcome.

Further complexity in the same approach can be added by considering situations in which each spouse might be unwittingly reinforcing unadaptive behavior in the other. Such was the case, for example, with Mr. and Mrs. Smith, described in Chapters 1 and 2. Here, Mr. Smith contributed to the maintenance of his wife's depressive behavior after being left alone by being extremely attentive to her. Further examples can be seen with Mr. and Mrs. Fisher, described in Chapter 3. The most obvious instance concerned Mr. Fisher's behavior of responding to his wife's fearful belief that she would harm others by locking up the "dangerous items," such as aspirin tablets, thus reinforcing her fears and beliefs.

We now describe a more complex case of marital conflict treated behaviorally. Mr. and Mrs. Baker, a 40-year-old couple with three children, sought help to resolve their conflict over Mr. Baker's irresponsibility with money, a situation which had brought them close to divorce. A second problem was Mrs. Baker's refusal to interact sexually with her husband, because she was so consistently angry at him that she was unable to become sexually aroused. Mr. Baker complained in turn that he received nothing but criticism from his wife. The only satisfaction he was able to get in life was through spending money, which he tended to do impulsively. Other difficulties included the fact that Mr. Baker was dominated and frightened by his mother, who would scold him by telephone every evening. Mrs. Baker found this extremely amusing and made fun of him about it. Mr. Baker, in turn, would make fun of Mrs. Baker's intense anxiety about riding in elevators, and would tease her every time the family waited together for an elevator. The Bakers also had some disagreements about how to manage their children.

The therapist began negotiations by asking each of them to identify one specific behavior that they would be willing to change within the next two days that would be reinforcing to their spouse. Mrs. Baker agreed to clean out a closet, even though she did not understand its relevance to Mr. Baker's needs and feelings. Mr. Baker agreed to develop a complete list of outstanding bills, a task that would make him extremely anxious since his wife became infuriated each time there was a bill that she had not anticipated. In further negotiations, Mr. and Mrs. Baker agreed to engage in specific behaviors which would be supportive of each other when each became anxious. They also agreed to engage in joint planning sessions regarding child management and a systematic step-by-step program in which they developed a budget and together planned their expenses to match their income. Interesting side effects of these negotiations included a marked decrease in the general unhappiness and acting-out of their children and an increase in Mrs. Baker's sexual receptiveness.

## Group Treatment

Marital conflicts can sometimes be treated successfully in a behaviorally oriented group therapy setting. A characteristic of behaviorally oriented therapy groups in general is that they are content- or problem-oriented. That is to say, the group focuses on the development of specific skills or deals with a specific problem that all participants share. Examples could include marital conflict, unassertiveness, fear of examinations, parenting skills, or airplane phobia. Whatever the shared need, the group members come together in order to learn specific procedures for meeting their needs and perhaps to practice these procedures in the group setting. Groups are usually of limited duration such as ten once-a-week, two-hour meetings, and are highly structured by the therapist, who develops and implements an overall plan for progressing through the various steps involved in the behavior change program.

Let us briefly compare this type of group with ongoing process-oriented psychotherapy groups. Ongoing psychotherapy groups tend to focus not on the content of a particular problem but on the interaction between group members, or the group *process*. In other words, as individuals discuss their own problems and respond to each other, the therapist observes and comments on the nature of the responding and relating. In this way, each group member is encouraged to perceive the particular interpersonal effect that he or she has on the others. The members are also encouraged to express their feelings and to reflect on the feelings expressed by other group members and their impact on the group.

In contrast, the behavior therapist does not utilize "group process" as a therapeutic tool, but focuses on these matters only if they are found to interfere with therapeutic progress, which is brought about by active structured learning. In a group approach to the behavioral treatment of marital problems, the focus of the group could be on one of several possible areas for structured change. For example, a group could be oriented toward the learning of effective communication skills. Another group might teach the type of skills which were taught to Mr. and Mrs. Baker as described above. Here, individuals are asked to identify behaviors that they would like their spouses to change. Each couple then negotiates a contract involving the performance of specific new behaviors, and the outcome is reported to the group by each couple at the following session. One advantage of group over individual treatment is that the couples serve as models for each other in demonstrating possible areas for change, and in providing norms by which to evaluate their own changes. Another important advantage of group behavioral treatment is that the members provide reinforcement for successful changes that others have made.

## Concluding Comment

In concluding the section on marital problems, we emphasize again that many problems which are presented by individuals have significant marital components. Behavior therapists are in a strong position to deal effectively with these situations because of two particular factors in their procedure. The first is their orientation toward searching for events in the patient's environment that may be triggering or maintaining the problem behaviors. The second is their orientation toward identifying as many people as possible from the patient's environment who can become involved in the treatment process. These change agents can assist in observation and record-keeping as well as in providing cues and reinforcers for new, adaptive behaviors.

# 7
# Managing Your Own Behavior

People have been managing their own behavior since the beginning of the human race. The self-discipline, or "will power," that a person needs in order to develop significant skills or achievements in a particular field is nowadays referred to by behavior therapists as self-management, or self-control. Areas in which the development and application of self-management skills are needed range from everyday activities, such as practicing to become a good guitar player or jogging for physical fitness, to the much rarer and infinitely more demanding task of training to become a concert pianist or running for national political office.

## What Is Self-Management?

What is meant by the self-management of behavior? We are referring to exactly the same principles of behavior change and management as described and applied in previous chapters of this book. The term *self-management* is employed when it is the individual who takes the initiative and responsibility for deciding what changes he wants to make and for planning and implementing the program to make them.

There are many behavioral problems for which professional help is needed in addition to self-management skills. It would be needed, for example, whenever a person's problems are accompanied by a significant amount of emotional upset that would make it difficult to sort out the relevant dimensions objectively. It would also apply when other people are significantly involved, or when the problem is complex and could involve a number of different and interrelated changes. However, there are many other behavior change situations in which it should be possible for a person to go ahead successfully with relatively little outside help. The necessary conditions are that he should know what to do; that is, what steps to carry out, and should be organized and consistent in his approach.

The most basic aspect of self-management is "self," in that the individual assumes responsibility for the behavior change program. The behaviors that people are interested in changing by self-management usually involve pleasures that are not good for them in the long run (for example, eating, smoking, or excessive TV watching), or else aversive or boring activities whose long-term consequences are desirable while the short-term consequences are not as interesting (for example, exercising or studying). In the former case, the aim would be to decrease the behavior; in the latter, to increase it. In both kinds of situations the behavior is currently being controlled by its short-term consequences, while the objective is to bring the behavior under the control of its long-term consequences.

The two basic aims of the behavior therapist in working with any problem behavior are to bring about the desired changes and to teach the patient the self-management skills that are necessary to maintain the changes at a stable level. Successful patients will probably also have learned some basic principles and behavior change skills that they can apply to other aspects of their lives.

These aspects could include other problem areas in the person's life, and also the enhancement of skills and potential in areas of special interest. Thus, the learning of self-management skills equips the person with increased flexibility in satisfying his needs, organizing his environment, and making life choices.

Critics of behavior therapy and behavior modification have believed that persons to whom behavior change procedures are applied are coerced and controlled, thereby reducing the extent to which they have control over their own affairs. Contrary to this viewpoint, behavior therapists believe that their procedures are more appropriately viewed as "humanistic," since they increase the patient's ability to determine his own destiny and fulfill his potential. The general approach which the behavior therapist uses to accomplish this goal is to help the person become fully aware of the specific ways in which he currently behaves and of the principles of learning by which he can change these behaviors if he so chooses.

### Analyzing the Problem Situation

As with any other behavior change project, the first step in a self-management program is to specify the behavior to be changed. This can either be a new behavior that the person wishes to learn, or an existing behavior that the person wishes to either increase or decrease in frequency. For problem behaviors that are to be decreased, the next step is to identify the antecedents or cues that trigger the behavior in question, and also the consequences, or reinforcers that are maintaining it. For situations in which behaviors are to be newly learned or increased in frequency, the task is to identify potential cues and reinforcers.

## Behavior Change Strategies

As we have stated above, the principles and strategies used in self-management are the same ones that are used when the changes are planned and supervised by a therapist. Because the range of behaviors that are amenable to self-management is limited, however, the strategies that can be realistically applied are also limited. They can be conveniently summarized in the following six categories.

1. Self-observation;
2. Stimulus control: rearranging environmental cues;
3. Response planning: rearranging environmental consequences;
4. Self-administered overt consequences;
5. Self-administered covert consequences; and
6. Adaptive self-statements.

We discuss each of the above strategies in turn and illustrate them with behaviors to which they have been successfully applied.

## Self-Observation

Once the person has specified the target behavior, it must be defined in a way that enables it to be observed and counted. Perhaps the most simple assessment procedure is to record instances of the behavior in note form. For example, a person who wished to become more assertive might write a sentence or two about each situation in which he would like to have been more assertive. A second procedure involves the use of a counter to keep a running tally of individual instances of the behavior. Examples could include fingernail biting, making critical statements, or compulsive "nervous habits" such as sniffing or coughing. A third method of self-observation and recording involves charting on a daily basis. This method could be applied to measures such as body weight, number of cigarettes smoked, or number of minutes spent studying. Daily charting is also used when running tallies are kept.

Self-observation is included as a self-management strategy because the simple observing and recording of a behavior sometimes serves to change its frequency in the desired direction. This usually refers to the reduction or elimination of unwanted behaviors. There are at least two possible explanations as to why simple observation would serve to change behavior. First, knowledge of the current frequency of the behavior provides the person with immediate feedback about his performance. If the person has set a specific criterion goal for satisfactory performance, his perception of the discrepancy between his actual behavior and his goal would serve to motivate change, and a reduction in the discrepancy would serve as a positive reinforcer for the change. The second explanation refers specifically to unwanted behaviors, and depends on the fact that many people are not aware of the full extent to which they engage in an undesired behavior such as fingernail biting or excessive eating. The full awareness of the actual extent of the behavior, gained through systematic observation, is aversive and serves to punish the behavior, reducing its frequency. These two explanations overlap somewhat, and in many cases both might be applicable.

Let us review the case of Mrs. Harris, a 29-year-old woman who had been treated in behavior therapy, together with her husband, for a problem involving conflict between them. Toward the end of treatment, she asked how to go about curing herself of fingernail biting through behavioral procedures. The therapist discussed alternative strategies with her, emphasizing that she could probably work on the problem on her own provided she was willing to engage in accurate observation and record-keeping.

At the next session, Mrs. Harris reported that she had purchased a supermarket counter and had kept an accurate count of instances of nail biting over a six-day period. She had had some initial difficulty in defining exactly what she meant by "biting": whether it should include (a) all instances of touching a finger to her mouth, (b) only instances of touching her nail to her teeth, (c) only instances of closing her teeth over a nail, or (d) only instances of biting off a fragment of nail. She had finally settled on the definition as any instance of touching her finger to her lips. In selecting this particular definition, Mrs. Harris was taking advantage of the principle that whenever an undesired behavior consists of a sequence of events, behavior change is usually most successful if it is interrupted early in the sequence.

Initially, Mrs. Harris was so unaware of biting her nails that she tended to recognize it only after she had completed the act, and many instances of biting were probably not recognized at all. Thus, her frequency count increased over the first three days from 43 to 87 bites per day, probably reflecting her increased awareness of the behavior. By the third day, she was satisfied that she was recording all instances of nail biting, and she was horrified to learn how frequently she did it. By the sixth day, however, the frequency had dropped to 46. Mrs. Harris was confident that she could decrease it even further just by recording accurately and aiming for a consistently lower total each day. She also found that she could confine her biting to the fingers of one hand, and then even further to just two fingers of that hand. By the end of the third week, she reported that she had stopped biting altogether, and that her husband had given her a great deal of approval for this achievement. It seems clear that the change in Mrs. Harris' nailbiting behavior was brought about mainly by observation and recording in conjunction with personal goal setting, assisted by the effects of social approval and cognitive procedures.

## Stimulus Control: Rearranging Environmental Cues

Behaviors which are strongly under the control of environmental cues can often be changed by rearranging the cues. Thus, self-management through stimulus control involves rearranging environmental cues or stimuli that trigger the problem behavior. A similar procedure was taught to Mrs. Osborn in attempting to reduce her overeating, as described in Chapter 2. In working with obese persons, rearranging environmental cues usually involves putting attractive food out of sight, making all food less accessible, staying away from food stores as much as possible, having only a small portion on the plate during meals, and eating only in one location in the house.

For a student trying to increase his studying time, an important application of stimulus control would be to remove all distracting cues that could trigger interfering behaviors. Thus, he would remove from the desk all books and notes except those which were actually being used. He would also remove his radio or TV from the work area, and would arrange with his spouse or roommate not to be interrupted.

A person who was attempting to stop smoking would remove all environmental cues that could trigger smoking, such as cigarettes, ash trays, and other smokers. A common strategy for smokers is to agree to smoke only in one room of the house. In behavioral language, the person would be deliberately labeling all the other rooms as representing cues for nonsmoking. In each of the problem behaviors described above, the person would probably engage in additional self-management strategies besides removing existing cues for undesired behavior or adding cues for desired behavior.

## Response Planning: Rearranging Environmental Consequences

In self-management through environmental response planning, arrangements are made for the desired behavior change to be reinforced. The essential element of response planning is that the person arranges for the consequences of the desired or undesired behavior to follow *automatically*. Once arranged, it is out of the person's direct control.

One common use of this procedure is the *behavioral contract*. Let us examine the case of a college student who had to complete a project with a rather short deadline. This student utilized response planning in the following manner. He divided the work to be done into eight sections, corresponding to the eight remaining evenings that were available for working. He then arranged with his girlfriend, whom he called every night, to ask him each evening whether he had completed the prescribed section of the work for that evening, and to hang up immediately if he had not. Behavioral or contingency contracts are often prepared in written form and signed by both persons involved. This topic is discussed further in Chapter 8.

Another self-management procedure involving environmental response planning which has been employed for many years is the use of the drug antabuse, already mentioned in Chapter 2, in the treatment of alcoholism. The immediate effects of antabuse last for about 24 hours. If any alcohol is consumed during that time, the person experiences extremely aversive consequences involving nausea and vomiting. Thus, by using this drug the person prearranges the consequences of drinking over a 24-hour period.

### Self-Administered Overt Consequences

Self-administered overt or external consequences are actions, either positive or negative, which a person performs immediately after he has engaged in the behavior of interest. An example can be seen in the college student described in Chapter 2 who made the agreement with himself not to watch TV until a certain amount of studying had been completed each evening. Promising yourself an ice cream cone when you finish an unpleasant chore, or an evening out if you work in the garden all day, are examples of the more casual use of self-administered external consequences. Here, the reinforcement is directly under the control of the individual, and it is most important for the person to first recognize fully that the agreement with himself involves the possibility that he will *not* receive the reward. Therefore, the reward must be something that the person is fully prepared to voluntarily forgo if it should turn out that way. A colleague of the authors made an agreement with himself that he would purchase a new camera if and only if he lost seven pounds in weight over a nine-week period. He signed a written statement that he would not purchase the camera for another six months if he failed to meet this requirement. Thus he specified his willingness to accept a less desired outcome (not having the camera immediately) that he would accept if he did not make the needed behavioral changes.

Self-administered overt consequences can also involve punishment for an undesired behavior. For example, a man who wanted to stop picking at his cuticles decided to place a mark with a "magic marker" on the back of his hand for each instance of picking, to be scrubbed off each evening. Because he was a very neat person, the marks were highly aversive to him. Another punishing event that has been used successfully is a thick rubber band worn around the wrist. The rubber band is snapped each time the undesired behavior is performed, and has the advantage of being constantly and immediately available.

An agreement should always be made as to how the behavior in question is to be measured. For example, if the behavior of concern is cigarette smoking, one convenient way would be to count the number of cigarettes remaining in the pack in use at a given time each day, and to keep a record of the number of packs purchased or taken out of the carton. Use of this procedure would also require an agreement not to take cigarettes from other people or to give them away.

### Self-Administered Covert Consequences

The use of covert self-statements (that is, thoughts) to reinforce desired behaviors is rather new in behavior therapy but promises to become a major contributor in bringing about significant changes. People constantly make statements to themselves about most things that they do. They positively reinforce themselves for desired behaviors ("I did that job well!"), and punish themselves for undesired behavior ("Boy, was that a stupid thing to do!"). Because the formal use of these procedures in behavior therapy is relatively new, the best ways to use them are not yet well understood. Covert reinforcers can also consist of visual images. To return to our earlier examples of smoking and excessive eating, people who can consistently punish the behavior of reaching for a cigarette or piece of chocolate cake with a visual image of dying under the surgeon's knife or gasping in the last throes of a heart attack will be able to substantially reduce these unwanted behaviors.

Most of us utilize covert behaviors as secondary reinforcers to tide us over until the primary reinforcer is available. The student who says to himself, "Only 40 more pages and I get to watch the football game" is employing self-statements as intermediate or conditioned reinforcers to bridge the gap to the primary reinforcement. Likewise, the politician must constantly keep a clear vision of his goal in mind in order to maintain his motivation while engaged in the tedious work of developing his campaign.

Some people make negative self-statements at a high rate no matter what they are doing. "I'll never be able to do this"; "Nobody loves me"; "My opinion isn't worth anthing" are some of the more common examples. Psychologist Albert Ellis was the first to point out that many people engage in such thoughts without being aware of doing so, and that these thoughts strongly influence feelings and overt behavior. In Ellis's rational-emotive psychotherapy, people are taught to pay careful attention to these irrational beliefs and to deliberately change them to more rational beliefs. A therapist's help is often essential in order to help the person recognize the unadaptive self-statements and to plan changes.

## Adaptive Self-Statements

Another new and important area of self-management involves the use of a therapist or trainer in teaching individuals how to engage in adaptive self-statements as a means of successfully overcoming a variety of difficulties. One increasingly common procedure is to combine adaptive self-statements with the use of existing pleasurable events as reinforcers. A pleasurable event is chosen that is reasonably automatic in the person's daily activity. Cues are then provided to trigger the adaptive self-statements immediately before the pleasurable event. The pleasurable event then follows immediately after the desired behavior and acts as a reinforcer for the desired behavior.

Let us consider the man who persistently believed that other people did not respect his opinions, even though there was good evidence that they did. In order to bring the content of his thoughts into line with reality, he devised a procedure for reinforcing the realistic thought by deliberately engaging in it immediately before a pleasant event. The pleasant event which he selected was lighting a cigarette, which he did about 25 times each day. He wrote the realistic self-statement, "People respect my opinions when I say what I think," on a small card which he inserted into the cellophane of his cigarette package. Each time he reached for a cigarette, the card served as a cue to trigger the self-statement, which he rehearsed covertly five times before lighting the cigarette. Over a one-month period, the frequency of this self-statement increased to the extent where he found that he did indeed have the "courage" to speak up and say what he thought. This new behavior resulted in direct positive reinforcement from the people with whom he spoke. Other events which have been successfully used as reinforcers in this manner include eating meals or snacks, starting to urinate, and driving off after stopping at a stop light. These examples also serve to illustrate the Premack principle, which refers to the fact that any high frequency behavior can be used to reinforce behavior of lower frequency.

Procedures involving adaptive self-statements have also been developed by psychologist Donald Meichenbaum for use in treating a number of different problem areas, including impulsive children, schizophrenic patients, and individuals with chronically high anxiety about a variety of situations. This self-instructional method involves learning to "think aloud" in adaptive ways, and then saying the same sentences silently rather than aloud.

In working with students suffering from high anxiety about taking examinations, the procedure might involve an imaginal situation in which the student is about to take a test. He would be instructed to make adaptive self-statements such as: "I'll just think about what I can do about it, that's better than getting anxious", or "I won't think about fear, just about what I have to do." Once these skills have been learned in a particular situation, they can be applied to other situations involving disruptive anxiety.

It is possible that over the next few years we will see the rapid development of ways of teaching generalized procedures for self-management aimed at training persons to learn how to apply sophisticated behavior change skills in all problem areas of their lives. As an example, Meichenbaum has described a possible extension of his work in which the person instructs himself to break down each task into small manageable steps, to remain calm if he is becoming anxious, and to concentrate on the immediate step at hand. In another procedure, which he has termed "stress inoculation," Meichenbaum has studied the effectiveness of combining these procedures with physical relaxation.

## Self-Management of Depression

Depression is a common problem to which self-management procedures are increasingly being applied. Most of the recently developed self-management procedures for depression do involve some professional assistance, but increasing amounts of responsibility and initiative are placed on the patient. It should be emphasized that not everybody is able to utilize these procedures without a significant amount of professional help. However, they represent innovative examples of what might be done.

Psychologist Barry Jackson, in working with a 22-year-old depressed housewife, found that she engaged in self-criticism at a high rate and rarely engaged in self-praise. Also, her personal standards for praiseworthy behavior were unrealistically high. The first step in treatment was to help her adopt more realistic standards for tasks such as household chores, so that she would be entitled more often to self-praise. The second step was to teach her to engage in self-praise following the successful completion of a task. Initially, she was taught to assign herself up to ten poker chips according to her evaluation of her performance. This procedure was combined with the use of more primary self-reinforcers, such as having a cigarette, calling a friend, or complimenting herself. Two months after termination of contact with the therapist, she was using self-reinforcement regularly and remained free of depressive thoughts.

Another procedure which also involves the development of a realistic self-evaluation and the use of self-reinforcement has been developed by psychologist Lynn Rehm, working in a group setting. As the first step, group members were taught to monitor their own behavior and in particular to keep track of all positive activities, defined as those that were pleasant or produced rewarding effects. In the second step, group members picked pleasant behaviors which they wished to increase and were taught how to set realistic subgoals as steps in attaining these final goals. In the third step, members were taught how to use self-reinforcement in attaining these goals. This group program, which extended over six weeks, was successful in significantly reducing depressive feelings.

In another program for the self-management of depression, designed by psychologist Roland Tharp, much less professional assistance was involved. The four women who participated in the program had all completed self-change projects on other, less complex behaviors. In working on depression, each person was simply told to use her knowledge to design her own treatment plan, and in doing so to pay particular attention to the antecedents of her depressive feelings. All four women showed objective evidence of being able to successfully modify their depression. One was able to do so simply by recording "good" and "bad" feelings related to individual activities during the day, and by using this information to perform more "good" activities. Two other women utilized self-reinforcement for noting and interrupting the stimuli that led to the depressive feelings. For one, reinforcement involved a favorite hobby, and for the other, a pleasant daydream. The fourth woman began a reinforcement program for making "honest" statements, which greatly increased their frequency and diminished the depressive feelings.

It is now apparent that some persons can successfully modify their own depressive difficulties with a minimum of therapeutic assistance. Researchers and theorists are constantly working on the further understanding and self-management procedures and on ways to reduce the need for professional assistance even further.

## Self-Management and Chronic Pain

One of the newest areas for the application of behavioral procedures is in the management of chronic pain. Because chronic pain is, by definition, a continuing problem that requires constant management, self-management procedures can be particularly important. In the most extensive behavioral analysis of this area, psychologist Wilbert Fordyce has divided the problem into two aspects: those involving respondent pain behaviors, and those involving operant pain behaviors.

*Respondent pain behaviors* are those that occur automatically when the body produces pain and are most effectively controlled by physiological procedures such as drugs. However, there are a number of interesting behavioral possibilities for reducing respondent pain behaviors. One new group of methods involves biofeedback procedures, discussed in Chapter 4. Other methods involve simple self-management. For example, it often happens that a part of the body in which chronic pain is experienced must be exercised regularly in order for optimal healing to occur. The natural procedure is to exercise until the pain becomes too great and then to rest. Such a procedure, however, reinforces the increased perception of pain, since rest (a negative reinforcer because of the pain reduction) is made contingent on reaching a certain level of pain. A more appropriate procedure is to set a reasonable quota for exercise (for example, 20 knee bends in five sessions today, increasing each day by one per session) and to fulfill the requirements of each exercise without regard to the degree of pain. Thus, the completion of the required behaviors is reinforced, and the perception of pain is not.

*Operant pain behaviors* are those that are shaped by the environment. Researchers now believe that in most cases of chronic pain, the majority of the pain behaviors are operant; that is, they are maintained by environmental consequences. Such behaviors can be divided into three groups. Some are directly reinforced with positive consequences. Crying is one example, since it almost always leads to sympathy. Most people are heavily reinforced as children for responding to pain in this manner. Other operant pain behaviors are negatively reinforced, through avoidance of aversive consequences. Thus, people often use their pain as an excuse to get out of undesired activities, thereby reinforcing the operant aspects of their pain behavior. Third, it sometimes meets the needs of the pain person's family members to maintain the person as "sick." This might be done, without realization, by failing to reinforce "well" behaviors, such as the actual performance of "well" activities or statements by the person that he feels much better today.

Because chronic pain is such a complex problem, professional assistance is necessary in most cases to develop new and adaptive behaviors, and the assistance of the person's entire family is also needed. However, the more directly the problem is approached within the framework of self-management, the more completely the person in pain can succeed in minimizing his difficulties.

## Self-Management and Natural Childbirth

In the last 10 to 15 years there has been rapid increase in the popularity of procedures which train pregnant women to approach the experience of childbirth as an active participant and without anesthesia. Perhaps the most popular training procedure is the one developed by the French obstetrician Fernand Lamaze. A typical Lamaze training package extends over six weekly two-hour group sessions, beginning around the seventh month of pregnancy. These training programs are essentially behavioral in nature and involve a considerable amount of self-management. An essential component of natural childbirth training is a partner or "coach," usually, but not necessarily, the husband, who is trained as a change agent. The woman is trained in a variety of needed skills, while the coach is trained to recognize the different situations in which each skill is needed, to note when the skills are being used properly, and to provide cues, instructions, and reinforcers for the woman in performing the skills.

The orientation of natural childbirth training is similar to behavior therapy in a number of ways. First, there is a client-consultant or instructor-student relationship between the natural childbirth instructor and each couple. Second, information giving is important. A thorough and complete account is given of the process of childbirth and of the likely and unlikely events that may occur. Third, systematic homework assignments and daily practice are required, and these continue until the baby is born. Fourth, the change agent is actually present during labor and delivery as an essential component of the procedure, taking part in the childbirth process exactly as trained.

Natural childbirth training relies on several basic behavior change processes. Substantial use is made of real-life desensitization to fears that are associated with childbirth and with the unfamiliarity of the procedures and surroundings. Desensitization procedures might include the following: (a) slides of a typical labor room; (b) slides of women in labor and their coaches; (c) slides of a typical delivery room and its equipment; (d) slides of women giving birth attended by their coaches and the medical staff; (e) a tour of actual hospital facilities where the woman is to give birth, including inspection of actual rooms and the nursery; and (f) extensive reading materials describing the application of natural childbirth procedures in actual cases. The desensitization procedures are enhanced by mutual reassurance of group members and by speakers who have already undergone the experience of natural childbirth.

Physical relaxation training procedures also play a central and important part in natural childbirth training. Intense physiologically generated pain is an unavoidable part of childbirth, since major bodily changes take place in the woman's pelvic area, mainly involving the vaginal muscles. The woman's "natural" reaction to this intense pain is to contract her muscles. Such a response is unadaptive for two reasons: it increases the pain, and it impedes the physiological changes. However, most women have never had occasion to pay systematic attention to their vaginal muscles and to learn how to relax them voluntarily. In order to teach these skills, with the aim of reducing the pain to tolerable levels, the woman is taught systematic general relaxation followed by differential relaxation of the vaginal muscles, including the ability to discriminate different degrees of tension in these muscles. The next step is to learn to associate a complex series of cues with relaxation and to practice the behaviors daily in the presence of the cues. Several kinds of cues are involved: verbal cues by the coach, physiological or kinesthetic cues, and portable visual or auditory cues which the woman takes with her to the hospital.

Another extensive set of skills taught to the woman consists of specific breathing patterns, for which the coach provides cues by counting slowly. The coach coordinates his cues with the onset and offset of contractions during labor. These complex breathing patterns serve two functions: they provide further cues for relaxation, and they are highly distracting and demand a great deal of the woman's attention, thus removing her focus from the pain. When labor is in progress, the coach selects the particular breathing pattern to be used according to the stage of labor that has been reached. Daily practice in the weeks before actual labor consists of systematic rehearsal of the different stages of labor and the relaxation and breathing patterns to be associated with each.

Many other behavioral processes might be identified in natural childbirth training, including the woman's cognitive self-statements of coping and mastery, and positive reinforcement provided specifically by the coach and in general by other persons in the hospital environment. The major and ultimate positive reinforcement, of course, is that of being awake and alert during the birth process and taking an active part in the experience of childbirth.

# 8

# Children: Parent and Teacher Consultation

The application of behavior therapy procedures to problems of children is rather different from traditional ways of working therapeutically with children. It is also somewhat different from behavioral approaches to the problems of adults. In working behaviorally with children, the therapist functions as a consultant, training and supervising parents and teachers, who serve as the primary change agents. In a small minority of cases the therapist might work directly with the child.

There are number of reasons for taking a consulting approach in working with children. First, at the time that treatment is sought, most of the problems experienced by children are being actively cued and reinforced by their environments, and these environments can neither be changed by the children nor directly by the therapist. A child's two major environments are the family and the school, which are under the control of parents and teachers, respectively. These adults are generally not aware that they are maintaining the very behaviors that they wish to change. Second, the cues and reinforcers for children's problem behaviors are usually easy to spot, since they tend to be rather recent. This can be contrasted with adults' problems, which have often been present for many years so that the cues have become obscured and the reinforcement might be highly intermittent and difficult to identify. Third, parents and teachers constitute instant, built-in change agents. Since they are available to work with the children a great deal of the time, their use is highly economical. The use of behavioral procedures to teach new adaptive behaviors takes no more time, and frequently less, than enduring the frequent hassles and conflicts that usually accompany problem behaviors. Since parents and teachers control children's behavior anyway, it would seem sensible to teach them to do the best possible job.

Problems of children cover a wide age range, from infancy to adolescence. Within a given age range, the personal capabilities of the children differ widely. For these two reasons, there is enormous variation in the extent to which a child can actively participate in his own treatment. Most readers will also be aware that the use of behavioral approaches with children is not confined to problem behaviors. It is also applied widely in dealing with everyday living situations and in teaching new skills. Of course, such procedures were utilized for many years before they were called "behavioral." Parents have given children pocket-money contingent upon keeping their beds made and rooms tidy, teachers have kept children after school for talking out of turn, and breakfast cereal companies have supplied a variety of reinforcers for opening a package of their particular product.

## Adult Problems and Children's Problems

In our discussion of marital problems in Chapter 6, it was stated that the couple often misperceives the source of the problem. One of the partners might be blamed when it is the other who is primarily maintaining the conflict, or when both are jointly making significant contributions. When children's problems are involved, the situation is even more complicated. It is common for parents to bring a child in for treatment for a problem which they see as residing within the child. Because the child's environment is set up and maintained primarily by the parents, however, they and indeed the entire family must be regarded as contributing in major ways to the problem. It is the behavior therapist's task to sort out exactly who is contributing to the problem, and in what manner.

Parents often expect to place their child in the therapist's hands to be cured, with their own involvement limited to periodic meetings to discuss progress. This "uninvolved" approach has been the norm in past years, but is much less so today. However, it is still common for many therapists to take the traditional view that most problems are within the child, and to undertake direct individual therapy aimed at helping the child resolve his difficuties. In this process, it is usual to use toys and games as a basis for developing a relationship between the child and therapist. The child's difficulties become exemplified within this relationship and are dealt with appropriately by the therapist as they occur. While the child is being treated, it is usual for the mother to be seen by another mental health professional in order to help her better understand herself and thus improve her relationship with her child.

The growing popularity of *family therapy* in the past decade reflects a recognition of the growing importance of the family environment for the problems of any one family member. Here, the family is seen as a unit, and the interaction among family members in the therapy setting is viewed as a sample of their typical interaction together. Thus, the child's problem environment is actively involved in the treatment process, and attempts are made to teach new skills that can be practiced outside the therapy session.

In the behavior therapy approach, this increased involvement is taken even further. The parents are taught in a formal manner how to change the child's environment in a way that will alleviate the child's problem behavior, and how to stabilize the new situation so that the desired changes become permanent. Thus, it is the parents who do the routine work of treatment, and some of the most important changes are those made by the parents in their own behavior. If the parents cannot be convinced that their full involvement is needed, the therapist will probably decline to work with the case.

Once the therapist has had an opportunity to examine the details of the problem, it can usually be viewed in one of three categories. First, the most serious aspect of the problem might involve a conflict between the parents which is not fully perceived by them. The child becomes a scapegoat and gradually comes to be regarded as the basic cause of the family's unrest. Such children rapidly develop very real problems of their own, and these problems are seized upon as evidence that it is indeed the child who is at fault. Often, if there are several children in the family, one child in particular becomes the scapegoat for parental difficulties.

The second category is that in which the parents recognize that they are playing a significant role in the child's difficulties, but they either do not understand exactly how they are doing it or they feel helpless to change the situation. Here, the parents acknowledge their own conflicts and wish to do something about them, recognizing that the family as a whole is being adversely affected. The third situation is that in which the child indeed has a very real problem, independent of the parents' adjustment. If the child's problem is a severe one, such as mental retardation or autism, the difficulties that are created for other family members are likely to create conflicts among them, adding an additional dimension to the child's problem.

Behavior therapy procedures with children, as with adults, involve some degree of trial and error. The therapist usually considers the most economical approaches first, provided they are consistent with the results of his behavioral assessment. An interesting example of a therapist's failure to take this approach and the resulting extra cost can be seen in the case of Mike, an eight-year-old boy from a low income family in an inner-city area. Mike suffered from the problem of encopresis (soiling his pants), which he would do almost every day while at school. The therapist systematically taught the mother basic principles of reinforcement, and then tried to identify reinforcers for the boy that were readily available to the parents. After a number of frustrating sessions with the mother, it occurred to the therapist to consider reinforcers that might be available to him but not to her. As a result, the therapist asked Mike to visit the clinic each afternoon on the way home from school if he was "clean" and to collect a quarter from the clinic secretary. The problem disappeared in two weeks, at a total cost, including follow-up, of approximately five dollars.

# Working with Parents and Children

We now review in detail the way in which the behavior therapist works with parents and children. The procedure can be divided into three general stages: initial assessment, information giving and training, and treatment and supervision. We illustrate each stage with an ongoing case example, a ten-year-old autistic boy named Jay, whose parents sought help in improving his speech skills. This case has previously been reported in an article by Sondra B. Goldstein and the senior author.

## Initial Assessment

The behavior therapist first seeks to obtain a detailed and accurate description of the nature of the problem as currently experienced and also of its development. This information is obtained in initial interviews with parents, which may be supplemented by the use of a structured self-report biographical data sheet or a problem checklist. The therapist uses this information in helping the parents to define the problem behavior or behaviors in a concrete manner, and works toward an agreement with the parents as to what specific changes are needed.

In the next stage of the initial assessment, which may overlap with the first stage, the parents are asked to begin making preliminary observations and taking systematic notes. These observations serve as a first step toward specifying the problem behaviors and identifying some of the important events (cues and reinforcers) associated with their occurrence. It is common, although by no means always necessary, for the therapist to see the child during the initial assessment period. The therapist is more likely to do so when the problem behaviors can be observed directly, as with Jay's articulation problem, to be discussed below. The interview may also serve the purpose of identifying contributions from factors such as physical difficulties or severe emotional problems that might not be recognized by the parents. The therapist should not overlook the possibility that a child's problem might be based in a need for glasses or a hearing aid.

There are two further steps in the initial assessment stage. The therapist discusses the nature of behavioral treatment with the parents and emphasizes the central and direct role which they will have as change agents for the child. The therapist also introduces the possibility that parental adjustment problems might be contributing in some manner to the child's difficulties, and evaluates this possibility by interview and perhaps with objective tests such as the Minnesota Multiphasic Personality Inventory.

**Example: The case of Jay.** We now illustrate the initial assessment stage with the case of Jay, as introduced above. Jay's parents were clear in their goals for treatment: to improve Jay's speech articulation to the point where he could be understood by others. The relatively few words which Jay currently spoke were incomprehensible to everybody except his parents, and this difficulty was a significant factor in limiting his progress in school and in his developing social skills.

In the therapist's first session with Jay's parents, a history of the problem was obtained. Jay, their first and only child, was a quiet, unresponsive baby who did not arouse suspicion until about one and a half years of age, when the parents noticed that he was not acquiring speech appropriately. They consulted a pediatrician for about one year and were informed that Jay was a "slow developer." At age three, Jay was taken to a child psychiatrist, who diagnosed him as autistic. A subsequent diagnosis at age six, based on psychological tests, labeled him as "possibly retarded with secondary emotional problems." Jay's parents tutored him at home from age seven to nine and then entered him in a school for emotionally disturbed children where he was currently performing at first-grade level.

Jay's parents reported that he displayed a number of disruptive behaviors, such as aimless gesturing, repeating meaningless phrases, refusing to let his mother change his room arrangement, and dropping objects down heating vents. However, they cited his unintelligible speech as the problem of concern, feeling that his schooling and social progress were being considerably retarded because neither his teachers nor peers could understand his speech.

At the second session the parents brought Jay to the clinic for an assessment of his speech and his disruptive behaviors in that environment. Jay's speech was indeed highly idiosyncratic, with only occasional words correctly articulated. He did respond to the question "What is this?" as the therapist held up objects, but most of his answers were impossible to understand. Next, Jay was observed by the therapist through a one-way window while interacting with his parents. Jay was much less hyperactive with his parents than with the therapist. He readily gave misarticulated names to all objects that the parents held up, and he cooperatively completed a simple form-board task. From these observations, the therapist concluded that Jay's parents would be able to gain sufficient cooperation from him to make possible a systematic shaping program for improving his speech.

To screen for the existence of psychological problems, both parents were asked to complete the Minnesota Multiphasic Personality Inventory. No obvious difficulties were apparent, although both parents responded in a rather defensive manner, making evaluation difficult. A brief paper-and-pencil intelligence test showed that Jay's mother was in the average range of intelligence and his father somewhat above average. To establish a baseline for Jay's current speech performance, the therapist asked the parents to compile over a two-week period a complete list of Jay's words and phrases that were intelligible to them.

Information Giving and Training

We now put aside the case of Jay, and return to a general description of the basic procedures that are followed in the next stage of the behavioral treatment of children. In this stage, the therapist seeks to impart to the parents all the information they will need in order to collaborate with the therapist in planning the treatment procedures and put these procedures into effect. Included would be basic information about behavioral treatment procedures in general, information about the nature of their child's specific disorder, and information about any interpersonal difficulties experienced by the parents that might be contributing to the disorder or that might tend to interfere with the treatment process.

Basic principles. Because the parents are to serve as the primary change agents, it is necessary for them to learn at least a minimal amount about behavior change procedures in general. Since the most common techniques in working with children involve simple reinforcement, the instruction usually includes an understanding of the principles of reinforcement, its effects on behavior, and practical skills in using it. The way in which this information is communicated to the parents depends on the motivational and intellectual level of the parents. For parents of at least average intelligence and motivation, there are a number of inexpensive books, such as *Living With Children* by Gerald R. Patterson and M. Elizabeth Gullion, which present the material in a structured manner with programmed format and/or proficiency exercises. It is most helpful if both parents become familiar with the material so that they can collaborate and check each other's understanding. The therapist urges the parents to make no attempt to apply the principles immediately, but to think of questions regarding concrete examples that would apply to them and their child, and to bring these questions in for discussion.

For parents who are not able or willing to gain this basic information by reading a book and discussing examples with each other and with the therapist, several alternative procedures can be used. For example, cassette tape recordings containing the basic information can sometimes be a viable method of learning. Or, the parents might be willing to attend one or more group sessions that are specifically designed to communicate the basic principles. As a last resort, the therapist might give the parents very simple step-by-step instructions about what to do at home, and would monitor them very closely to ensure that they were doing it correctly. Such a procedure might be used, for example, with a multi-problem family where the parents are overwhelmed with difficulties but where certain rather simple changes might lead to significant improvement in the child. It might also be used with parents of limited motivation or intelligence.

**Nature of the disorder.** A second area of information which the therapist makes available to the parents involves the nature of the child's difficulty and what is known about it scientifically. Once again, the information is often vital in successful treatment, although the way in which it is communicated will depend on the motivational and intellectual level of the parents. At the least, the parents need to know, for example, that a child with a simple phobia can usually be treated successfully in a straightforward manner, while a child diagnosed as autistic has a major and serious disorder in which treatment progress is painfully slow. Such information helps parents to form realistic expectations about what can and cannot be accomplished in treatment and gives them added sophistication in recognizing aspects of the problem and discussing them with the therapist.

**Parents' problems.** The third kind of information that should be communicated to the parents involves the parents themselves and their interaction with the child's difficulties. It is here that the therapist needs the greatest degree of skill, so that the stage can be set for the parents to work productively with the child, while negative reactions, such as anger, denial, self-blame, or premature termination of treatment, can be kept at a minimum. If the parents' problems are ongoing, are only dimly recognized by them, and are directly contributing to the child's difficulties, the therapist might suggest that these problems be approached first and before a serious effort is made to change the child's behavior. It is rare to encounter parents who view their child's difficulties without some denial, on the one hand, or inappropriate self-blame, on the other. Thus, it will nearly always be necessary at least to review with the parents the different ways in which their behavior could be interacting unproductively with the child's and to help them make appropriate changes.

Continuing assessment. The therapist continues with the task of having the parents accurately pinpoint the precise behaviors to be changed and gather systematic information on the frequency of these behaviors. In some situations, such as Jay's articulation problem, the behaviors are adequately defined when they are initially introduced by the parents. In many other cases, however, parents may have only a vague notion of what should be changed. Or, they may make a clear statement but fail to recognize the complexity of the situation or realize that the problem cannot be solved as simply as they would like.

If the problem behaviors are easy to define and are readily agreed upon by parents and therapist, the parents are instructed to begin making systematic observational records in the same way as discussed in Chapter 1 for adult problems. The most appropriate type of observational procedure depends on the problem, but often involves a simple frequency count and careful notes about the consequences, or ongoing reinforcement, for the behavior.

If the problem behaviors are not yet pinpointed, the parents are asked to continue keeping careful records of the behaviors they believe to be the problem or that are related to the problem. Forcing them to attend closely to the problem environment in this manner generates the information needed for further discussion between parents and therapist aimed at specifying precisely what is to be changed. It is often necessary for parents to keep records for several weeks, testing their ideas and discussing difficulties with the therapist, before arriving at a workable definition of the problem behavior for purposes of behavior therapy.

An important but often overlooked aspect of the parents' observational task is to have them also observe and keep records of *positive* behaviors, those behaviors that the parents would like the child to perform more frequently. Because parents tend to focus most often on undesirable behaviors, positive behaviors are often overlooked, and the parents' attitude toward the child and his ability to change is usually quite negative. By having the parents become aware that there are some positive behaviors that the child currently performs and that can be increased fairly readily, the therapist can more easily convince them that change is possible and under their control. The reader is reminded once again that an undesirable behavior can often be eliminated by focusing instead on the task of increasing an incompatible, desirable behavior.

**The case of Jay.** Let us now return to Jay and his parents. It is unusual to encounter parents who already have a basic working knowledge of behavioral principles as applied to behavior change in children. Jay's parents, however, did have such a knowledge, which they had gained through their association with the local chapter of a national organization for parents of autistic children. It was this background that had played a major part in prompting them to seek more complete consultation. The parents had somewhat less information about autism, and they harbored substantial and pervasive feelings of guilt about Jay's condition, believing that they were directly at fault in some way that they did not yet understand.

To deal with the parents' guilt, the therapist provided them with realistic information about autism. This included the fact that the cause or causes of autism have yet to be discovered, and the therapist's personal belief that an organic basis for the disorder would ultimately be found. The parents were very relieved to hear these views, and became much more open in their communication. After further discussion regarding the parents' needs and expectations, the therapist judged that they were realistic in their immediate goals for Jay. However, because they had given little thought to long-range plans for managing Jay, the therapist warned them that progress with autistic children is very slow and that expected gains often do not eventuate.

In view of the parents' intellectual level and their high motivation, the therapist concluded that they would be able to take advantage of direct reading materials related to treatment. The therapist therefore introduced them to the reinforcement and modeling procedures that had been used successfully in working with speech problems of autistic children by giving them copies of several journal articles which described these procedures in detail. The parents were asked to read the materials carefully and make note of any points that they did not understand.

As requested in an earlier meeting, the parents had made a list of words that Jay spoke over a two-week period. The completed list contained 90 words, nearly all of which were intelligible only to the parents. After discussion, the parents and therapist together agreed on two specific goals of treatment: (a) to make these 90 words intelligible; and (b) to add enough additional words to Jay's vocabulary so that simple social communication would be possible.

### Planning and Rehearsal

We return once again to our general discussion. Let us review the steps that have been covered to date in the behavior therapy process. By this point, the therapist has assessed the problem, including the parents' contribution, if any, and has given the parents information about behavioral procedures in general, the nature of the child's problem, and their own contribution to it. The therapist has helped the parents to adjust their emotions in order to deal with the situation as it realistically is and has asked the parents to begin gathering specific information about the precise problem behaviors involved.

If the exact behaviors to be changed have still not been pinpointed by this time, they must be pinpointed now. The parents and therapist together examine the notes that the parents have made about the specific problem behaviors, and agree on one or more behaviors that need to be increased or decreased. These must be behaviors that can be reliably observed by the parents; for example, eating meals without whining, lying, noncompliance with reasonable requests, surliness, fear of the water, or nightmares. An essential part of the process is defining exactly what the behavior is; for example, a nightmare might be defined as having occurred if the child wakes up crying and says that he has had a bad dream; lying might be defined as a situation in which the parents are "reasonably certain" that the truth was not told.

Having pinpointed the problem behavior and gathered data on its frequency, the therapist and the parents discuss specific expectations regarding the goals of treatment. If the problem is use of obscene language, for example, several alternatives could be considered as goals: (a) no obscene language whatever in the presence of the parents; (b) no more obscene language than average for children of that age; (c) no more than two instances of obscene language per month. Once the goal is agreed upon, there is an implied contract between parents and therapist. One further aspect should be discussed: the approximate length of time that treatment will take. The therapist gives his best estimate, and also indicates his confidence in this estimate. Because parents often grossly underestimate, and less often grossly overestimate, the amount of time and effort required, it is important for the therapist to be as specific as possible regarding these expectations.

By this time the therapist has a clear idea of the alternative methods that are available for bringing about the desired changes. He has also assessed the parents' ability and motivation as change agents, and is able to make a subjective assessment regarding the relative merits of different approaches. The therapist explains each approach to the parents at a level that they can understand and specifies what would be required of them in each.

Once they have agreed on a course of action, the therapist's next task is to train the parents in the needed behavior change skills. This training can range from 30 minutes of simple instruction to several weeks of detailed rehearsal with daily practice sessions at home. For example, if it is planned to increase a desired behavior through positive reinforcement, the task must be broken down into its component steps: selecting an appropriate reinforcer; deciding on the quantity of reinforcer to use; perhaps breaking down the desired behavior into small steps to be taught one at a time; discussing with the child the desired behaviors and the available consequences; providing for feedback from the child; and following through on the consequences. The parents and therapist usually rehearse the entire sequence one or more times until all are comfortable that it can be performed properly.

**The case of Jay.** We now return to our example of Jay's articulation problem. The therapist has already made the tentative judgment that a modeling-and-reinforcement procedure would probably be the most effective, and has selected several journal articles describing these procedures for the parents to read. It was decided to work first on the words which Jay misarticulated. The criterion for success was to be five consecutive utterances of the word in a manner that could be understood by a stranger. The therapist and parents together rehearsed different degrees of misarticulation until all agreed on the criterion.

Small portions of Jay's evening meal were chosen as the reinforcement for correct articulation. Since Jay's midday meal was provided at school and he received no afternoon snacks, he was usually quite hungry by supper time. The meal was cut up into small portions before the training session. At the mother's suggestion, a warming plate was used to keep the food hot throughout the session. Since the parents were concerned that Jay might not earn enough food to meet his health needs, it was decided to offer him a nonpreferred but nutritious food (oatmeal) three hours after the termination of a session in which he did not earn more than half of his regular meal. The family kitchen table was chosen for the site of the training sessions. The food plate was initially located directly in front of the parent, but Jay's tendency to reach for unearned food made it necessary to place the plate on a small table by the parent's side.

Seated opposite Jay, one of the parents would begin a training session by placing a portion of food on a spoon and holding the spoon at chin level. Since Jay would tend to look at the food, the position of the spoon ensured that he would be looking toward the parent's face. The parent was to wait until Jay's glance shifted from the spoon to the face, and then say the stimulus word for Jay to imitate. When Jay responded with an acceptable imitation, the parent would immediately say "Good" while placing the spoon in Jay's mouth. The verbal reinforcement served to bridge the time between Jay's utterance of the correct response and his receipt of the reinforcement, and would thus become a conditioned reinforcer for future use.

The word to be imitated was presented every four or five seconds. Whenever Jay said the word correctly, he was reinforced. Mild disruptive behaviors (leaving the chair, looking around) were gradually eliminated by removing all possible positive reinforcers for these behaviors. Thus, the parents would simply look away from Jay whenever mild disruptive behavior occurred. When Jay was again sitting quietly in his chair, the parent would reinforce this behavior by attending to him and proceeding with the session.

For rehearsal purposes, the parents indicated their willingness to bring Jay to the clinic together with his evening meal. The therapist first modeled the therapeutic behaviors for the parents; then each parent engaged in the behaviors in turn and was given feedback by the therapist. The parents offered to make tape recordings of their few sessions at home to enable the therapist to provide further feedback.

## Treatment and Supervision

The reader should understand by this point that it is the parents who are the clients, rather than the child. Essentially, the parents and the therapist have together designed a program to initiate and maintain changes in the parents' behavior. Thus, the progression of treatment is essentially the same as for a therapist working with any other adult. The therapist asks the parents to keep systematic records of their behavior and the child's, and uses these records to determine whether the desired changes are occurring or if the procedure should be modified or redesigned.

**The case of Jay.** We follow the treatment of Jay further as his parents engaged in the modeling-and-reinforcement procedure that the therapist taught them. The parents were instructed to keep a notebook on each day's training, in which they recorded the new and review words used in each session and also made other comments and observations. During a typical weekly supervision session, the therapist and the parents listened to parts of the tape recordings and reviewed the written notes. The parents brought up any specific problems they had noted and solutions were sought in joint discussion. On several occasions the parents brought Jay and his supper to the clinic and conducted a training session while the therapist watched through the one-way window. With the use of the tape recordings, however, it was not necessary for these visits to be frequent.

During the first 30 training days, Jay's rate of acquisition of correctly articulated words was approximately one word every three days. At this time, the parents expressed discouragement with Jay's slow progress, and the therapist suggested two changes. First, the parents were encouraged to stop using difficult three- and four-syllable words such as macaroni and refrigerator; second, any word not learned in five consecutive training sessions was to be dropped and perhaps reintroduced at a later date. After these changes were made, Jay's rate of learning doubled over the next 30 days, to approximately two words every three days.

On training day 75, when Jay had acquired 37 correctly articulated words, *labeling training* was introduced and was continued to day 100. The parents divided the 45-minute session into two periods, with 25 minutes of articulation training and 20 minutes of labeling training. The labeling training was role-played in detail by the therapist and parents. Thirty pictures of common objects such as a shoe, rug, and kite, whose names Jay could not initially articulate, were chosen from an illustrated second-grade reading chart. The parents held up a picture of an object, held the spoon of food directly beneath the picture, and asked "What is this?" When Jay looked at the picture, the parent prompted with the name of the object. Jay was reinforced for imitating the prompt. Gradually the time between the question and prompt was lengthened to five seconds or more. If Jay waited for the prompt, a partial prompt was given; for example, "shh" for shoe. Jay learned to label all 30 pictures correctly in 25 training days. In addition, the parents spontaneously began to question him about names of objects outside the training sessions, and reported that he was now readily imitating and learning the names of objects in the house and garden.

On training day 100 the parents began to require Jay to answer the question "What do you want to eat?" with the simple sentence "I want milk (potatoes, bread, etc.)" before he received his reinforcement. At the time of training day 125, the last formal session monitored by the therapist, the parents reported that Jay had learned to articulate correctly 83 words, all of which he grossly misarticulated at the beginning of training. He had also learned to label 30 pictures of objects and to express his food preferences appropriately in the sentence "I want . . . ." Perhaps most important, he had also made many gains outside the training sessions. Whereas he previously avoided talking at school, his teachers reported that he was now initiating simple conversations and seemed to be much more interested in communicating. Jay's parents noted his new willingness to answer their questions and his tendency to correct his own misarticulation of some words.

## Contingency Contracting

Earlier in this chapter we indicated the importance of involving the child in the process of therapy by discussing the proposed procedures and asking for feedback. These steps are often formalized into a structured procedure involving negotiations and a specific agreement, sometimes in writing. Such a procedure is called contingency contracting. Contingency contracting can be utilized with all people whether they have problems or not, and is no different in principle from any other kind of contract. It tends to be most useful to behavior therapists when working with children and particularly adolescents, when used either by the therapist directly or by teaching the skills to parents or school teachers. Contingency contracting has also been employed with parents to increase the probability that they will engage in such needed behaviors as keeping their appointments, returning borrowed materials on time, and doing their homework assignments.

As most readers will recognize, parents have been negotiating contracts with their children for many years, well before the development of behavior therapy as a formal field. What is different in the procedures as currently used, however, is that they are taught to the parents in a structured and systematic manner. A major contribution of behavior therapy has been to identify clearly the underlying principles, to specify how they can be most effectively used, and to identify the behaviors that interfere with their successful application.

The essentials of contingency contracting are as follows. The first step is to select one or two behaviors for which change is to be attempted. Parents and therapist must agree on the exact definition of these behaviors and on a specific method of observing and counting them. The next step is to identify positive reinforcers to be used in increasing the behaviors. Next, if the behaviors are performed at a time or place where the parents or teachers cannot keep track of them, it is absolutely essential to recruit somebody else who is willing to be trained to do the observation and recording. Such a person might also dispense the reinforcer.

The tentative plan as formulated so far is next discussed by the parents with the child, and specific aspects of the contract are negotiated until it is satisfactory to both child and parents. For example, the child might prefer TV watching as a reinforcer instead of extra allowance money or staying up later in the evening. Or, the child might point out that the behavior to be required is unreasonable and ask for several smaller steps. When there is complete agreement, the details of the contract are written down and signed by both child and parents as a commitment and an indication that the terms are agreed upon. The next step is to implement the contract for a short period of time that is agreed upon in advance, perhaps a week. The parents collect actual data on the child's behavior during this time and provide the reinforcers. If the child's behavior does not change, the parents and therapist "troubleshoot" the system to see where revisions are needed. The contract is then rewritten in consultation with the child. If the troubleshooting reveals that the parents did not carry out their part of the agreement, the contract is left in its original form and the therapist reemphasizes the necessity for their full participation. The process of monitoring, troubleshooting, and rewriting continues until the desired behavior changes have been accomplished.

Many behavior change systems for working with children make use of "points" which are earned and saved toward a specific reinforcer. Because the points acquire reinforcing power of their own, they can be termed conditioned reinforcers. Back-up reinforcers, such as going to the circus, roller skating, or buying a toy, can be made contingent upon the child's earning a certain number of points during the week. These points may be earned through a single activity or perhaps a combination of desired behaviors as designated by the parents. Much more complex point systems are used in token economy procedures, to be discussed in Chapter 9.

## Individual Problems in the Classroom

Teachers frequently encounter problems in the classroom to which simple behavior change procedures can be fruitfully applied. The single most widely used procedure is simple positive reinforcement, and the rules and principles for applying it are the same as those we have discussed above for parents. The most satisfactory approach is to train the teachers in basic principles of behavior. Since it is the teachers' professional responsibility to work with children's behavior, including problem behaviors, they are often willing to devote more time and effort than parents to learning these principles and procedures.

Because classroom teachers are required to respond to the needs of many persons, it is necessary for them to be particularly sensitive to the policies and values held by the school administrators and by the professional counseling and guidance personnel in the school. School systems differ widely in their policies for handling problem children and in the extent to which teachers are permitted the freedom to utilize their own preferred procedures. In general, the schools in which behavioral procedures are most successfully used are those in which they are actively accepted and encouraged by the administrative staff and the counseling and guidance personnel.

## Working Directly with Children

It is relatively unusual for a professional behavior therapist to work with a child directly. Because children's problems tend to be dependent on their environments, it is more economical for the therapist to work instead with the persons who have the greatest amount of control over their environments. However, there are some instances in which the behavior therapist might work directly with the child. Most of them involve situations in which the child has a *deficit* in skills and where the therapeutic techniques of choice require a high degree of skill. Skill deficits might have come about because the child has another more basic deficit, such as minimal brain damage, that has prevented him from learning the skills in the normal course of events. In other cases, the child's environment might not have provided normal opportunities for learning the skills in question. In either case, the first step taken by the behavior therapist would be to assess the environment to ensure that nothing would interfere with the learning of the needed behaviors, and to determine whether potential reinforcers are already available or whether they need to be developed and built into the environment.

An example of direct work with a child might involve the problem of impulsive behavior in which a child has never learned to engage in appropriate thoughts to accompany and monitor his actions. The behavior therapist might utilize the procedures described in Chapter 5, in which the child is systematically taught to "talk to himself" while performing a simple set of practice behaviors, as a first step in learning how to monitor his actions with thoughts. Another situation in which the behavior therapist might work directly with children would be in a group setting for developing social and interpersonal skills. The use of a group would enable the children to rehearse these new behaviors with other group members and to receive reinforcement from each other.

## Aversive Procedures

There has been little agreement among experts over the years about the extent to which children should be punished as a way of controlling their behavior. During the Victorian era it was traditional for parents to use direct punishment procedures as their primary method of control. Beginning in the 1930's, however, and due mainly to the influence of Sigmund Freud, punishment gradually gave way to the "permissive" era, in which children were encouraged more and more to do just about anything they wished. Since no alternative form of control was substituted for punishment, however, this approach also tended to be unsatisfactory. Behavior theorists now understand that a person's first response to punishment is to learn to do whatever will avoid the punishment, and that this new behavior might not necessarily be an adaptive one. In addition, punishment has undesirable side-effects, including anxiety and various specific physiological difficulties. Thus, direct punishment alone is usually not an effective way to control behavior, and does not deal with the child's need to learn appropriate new behaviors.

The use of mildly aversive procedures for weakening inappropriate behaviors in conjunction with a positive reinforcement program for strengthening appropriate behaviors is usually effective if it is properly designed. It should be recognized, however, that children regard most forms of control as aversive even if based in major part on positive reinforcement. The following practical rules provide guidelines for the appropriate use of aversive procedures. First, the desired behaviors that will be positively reinforced should be made known to the child so that he can make a choice. Second, corporal punishment should be avoided. Third, the reasons for control should be explained to the child and should be stated in terms of the wants and needs of the parents. Statements making the child feel guilty should be avoided.

One mildly aversive procedure that is often effective as part of a procedure for reducing the frequency of undesired behavior is known as *time-out*. Time-out procedures involve removal of the opportunity for the child to receive reinforcement for a specified short period of time. Usually, the child is physically removed from the situation whenever the undesired behavior occurs. Such procedures are not new with behavior therapy, of course; children have traditionally been sent to their rooms or made to stand in a corner or stay after school as a form of behavior control. The difference between these traditional procedures and time-out procedures is that the latter are employed within a structured plan to provide the most effective possible behavior change. For example, they are used in conjunction with a positive reinforcement program to encourage learning of desired behaviors. Another difference is that time-out periods are quite short; for example, five minutes rather than an hour. A third difference is that in time-out the contingency is explained in advance to the child and is done without anger. Finally, the behavior therapist using time-out makes sure that all potential reinforcers are removed from the time-out environment, and, in particular, that the time-out contingency itself is not a reinforcer by constituting an escape from a more aversive situation.

# 9

# Systems and Institutions

In this chapter we describe the application of behavior change principles in treatment programs within institutions and other group settings. These applications often involve large-scale programs covering many or most behaviors in the setting, and are designed so that the same rules apply to all members, with provision for individual flexibility. The staff members in these settings are usually given formal training for the special role of working within a behaviorally based program.

## Psychiatric Hospitals

The beginnings of behavior therapy in institutional settings took place in state psychiatric hospitals around 1960 with the application of simple positive reinforcement procedures in an attempt to change long-standing personal difficulties. Staff members were often astonished to discover that behaviors that were presumed to be chronic and permanent, such as meaningless talk and long periods of pacing or sitting, could be changed rather quickly. In some of the original research reports, chronic patients who habitually said little or nothing were taught to talk and be sociable; patients whose speech was normally garbled and incomprehensible started to talk clearly, patients who had to be spoon fed began to eat by themselves, and patients who engaged in unusual behaviors such as hoarding items on the ward were taught to stop.

One project, carried out by psychologist Teodoro Ayllon, involved a patient named Anne. For the previous 16 years Anne had refused to eat unless a nurse led her to the dining room, arranged the meal for her, urged her to eat, and at times spoon fed her. Ayllon reasoned that because food is a strong natural reinforcer, it should be possible to teach her to eat independently. Therefore, the ward staff set out to teach her successive approximations to independence in eating. At first the nurses were instructed to help her only after she had entered the dining room. After a slow start, Anne began going to the dining room alone, and in five or six weeks was going alone most of the time. The frequency with which she gathered her own tray, silverware, and food also increased from almost never to about 40 percent of the time, but not to 100 percent. Therefore, at week 21, all help in the dining room was discontinued. Within several days Anne was helping herself regularly, and two years later was still displaying normal eating behavior. The reader might note that results would probably have been more rapid if the ward staff had initially helped her in all but the final behavior of putting food in her mouth. This principle of working backward from the last step in a sequence of behaviors is illustrated more fully later in the chapter.

### Token Economies

Psychologists soon began to see the potential of behavioral technology using simple positive reinforcement for bringing about massive improvements in the lives of chronic psychiatric patients. Complex systems were gradually developed which used points or tokens rather than direct primary reinforcement. The tokens could be exchanged later for a variety of primary or backup reinforcers. Although the original use of token economy systems was mainly to make long-term residents of state hospitals more comfortable and socially appropriate, the emphasis gradually changed toward teaching patients the skills needed for living outside the hospital.

Token systems of reinforcement have a number of advantages. The delay between the desired behavior and the primary reinforcement is bridged. Tokens are portable and are continuously in the patient's possession. The number of tokens given can be in proportion to the amount of reinforcement that is merited. They can be cashed in for a wide variety of back-up reinforcers, and they allow patients to be reinforced without interruption of their ongoing behavior. The reader will readily see that most of the desirable properties of tokens are also possessed by our universal token system, money.

The development of token economy programs began in the early 1960's, about the same time as the whole philosophy of mental hospital care was changing in line with the new emphasis on locating mental health treatment in local community settings rather than in large isolated hospitals. Thus, there was considerable impetus for the development of any technique that was consistent with the goal of returning patients to their own communities.

In establishing a token economy system, a careful study is first made of the patients that are to be involved, noting the problems which they share in common. For a ward of chronic or long-term residents of a state hospital, there are usually two main kinds of problems, both involving skill deficits. The first are basic *self-help* skills, such as dressing appropriately, personal hygiene, attending meals on time, and making one's bed. The second are basic *interpersonal* skills, such as responding to a greeting, saying "Thank you," playing card games, watching TV with others, and talking about topics other than oneself.

The next step is to decide upon the primary reinforcers to be used, and what each will cost, in tokens. Also to be decided is the number of tokens to be paid for desired behaviors as listed above. In the early days of token economy programs, one of the most commonly used primary reinforcers was food. Patients were expected to purchase their meals with tokens earned by engaging in the most basic human behaviors. In more recent years there has been debate among psychologists and other members of the public concerning the goals and ethics of behavior therapy programs in psychiatric hospitals and the basic rights of patients. These debates have led to the redesigning of some reinforcement systems so that the tokens purchase items beyond the basic necessities of life.

Perhaps the most basic factor of all in the success of a token economy program is the active cooperation of the senior administrative staff of the hospital. Because the nature and routine of a ward run on token economy lines is very different from a typical hospital ward, administrative support is absolutely essential. An early step in developing a token economy program is usually to arrange a series of seminars or lectures for the entire hospital staff, in which the basic concepts of behavior are explained and the idea of an entire ward run on these principles is discussed. Because the staff that will work on the ward needs specialized training in behavioral technology, these sessions provide a good opportunity to identify nurses and other staff members who might be interested in this new experience. The entire staff of the ward must function as a team of behavior change agents, all following the same procedures as consistently as possible. The work is obviously demanding, and not all hospital personnel are either capable of it or interested in it.

**Levels of Functioning**

It soon became apparent to psychologists running token economy programs that their patients were on so many different levels of competence that several systems were required rather than just one. For example, for a "regressed" and socially isolated patient, watching TV would be a behavior that the staff would be delighted to see and would want to reinforce. Attending meals on time and eating unassisted might be another. For patients functioning at a more advanced level, however, their basic eating behavior would probably be taken for granted, and it might be decided to discourage too much TV watching in favor of taking part in structured social activities. For such a patient, TV watching would be a reinforcer for other behaviors.

For these reasons, most token economy programs developed a "levels" system. Patients at the most basic level might be those who needed to learn basic self-care and interpersonal skills, which for men might involve, for example, having one's shirt buttoned and tail tucked in, pants zippered and buttoned, face and hands washed, and hair combed. Reinforcers might include such events as going outside the ward, lying on the bed for a short period during the day, and TV watching. At an intermediate level, reinforced behaviors might include appropriate social conversation, speaking up in therapy groups, and volunteering to help on the ward. Reinforcers could include preferred food and sleeping quarters, visits to the canteen, and permission to leave the hospital for short periods. At the third and perhaps highest level, reinforcible behavior might include taking responsibility for ward activities and for other patients, and engaging in active planning behavior for one's own future. Reinforcers might include weekend home passes, access to a special lounge or day room with preferred accommodations, and unsupervised access to all parts of the hospital.

A "levels" program has several important aspects. First, patients are promoted to the next level according to a predetermined set of criteria that are made known to all patients, and involve demonstration of adequate functioning at the current level. "Adequate functioning" is usually defined as the behaviors and activities that are being reinforced at that level. If the system is properly designed, each patient is placed at the particular level that contains the behaviors which he is capable of learning and reinforcers which are motivating for him. Second, each succeeding level involves increasing amounts of behaviors and responsibilities of a social nature, and the reinforcers are also of an increasingly "social" nature.

Such programs can be developed even further to provide comprehensive rehabilitation experiences. One program, described by psychologist John Atthowe, has been in effect at the Veterans Administration Hospital in Palo Alto, California. In this program, containing three basic levels, patients could "earn" their way out of the token system altogether and into a sheltered workshop on the hospital grounds. Beyond this point, there were opportunities to take jobs off the hospital grounds such as gardening and operating gas stations, some of which paid wages comparable to any nonhospital work position. Thus, the graded system of tokens and levels was gradually merged into the same graded system of work activities and corresponding monetary rewards that exists for all of us.

Tokens and their back-up reinforcers were gradually "thinned out" over the levels and replaced with more natural reinforcers, such as regularly earned money, social status, comradeship, and self-reliance. Together with these changes, such patients were given the opportunity to buy their way into more private living quarters in the hospital and into a special self-help ward run mainly by the patients themselves. Some also had the opportunity to buy their way into houses off the hospital grounds, rented by small groups of patients. In all aspects of the patients' progression toward independence and self-sufficiency, steps were small, the options were clearly portrayed, the choices were made by the patients themselves, and the opportunity to "fall back" safely was always available. Contrary to traditional criticisms that behavioral programs are coercive and rigid, step-wise programs such as we have described use structured behavioral procedures in a humanistic and flexible manner to help increase patients' life opportunities, self-determination, and flexibility in making their own decisions.

## Community Mental Health Centers

As the focus of mental health treatment has moved over the last fifteen years from the state psychiatric hospital to decentralized community-based mental health and human service centers, so behavior therapy programs have been developed for the community-based treatment of persons with significant mental health problems. Let us review the experiences of one such program, the Oxnard Community Mental Health Center in California, as described by psychiatrist Robert Liberman. The Oxnard staff introduced a "coupon" system into the therapeutic program of their Day Treatment Center, a unit which provides a daily program for persons who do not need to be in a hospital full time but who require extensive professional attention during the day.

The coupons had the same purpose as tokens, and were used routinely to reinforce promptness of arrival at the Center and various maintenance tasks. These tasks, which were part of the cooperative structure of the Center, included preparation of meals, cleaning up afterward, general tidying up, and preparing for workshop and other treatment programs. Back-up reinforcers included extra consultation with the professional staff, preferred foods, bowling, bus trips, and free time. The coupon system was run largely by the patients, who met weekly to review the system and adjust rates and prices as necessary. In this token economy system, as in others, social reinforcement was paired with the giving of tokens. Thus, a staff member might say: "You did a nice complete job of cleaning up—here are your four coupons." The verbal statement, in addition to containing praise, specifies exactly what behavior is being reinforced.

After the system had been in operation for two years, the staff developed and implemented an improved system involving credit cards. Now, instead of actually receiving coupons, a small hole would be punched in the patient's weekly credit card signifying that he had earned credit for the coupons. As they were spent, a larger hole would be punched over the original hole, thus placing on the card a permanent record of the transaction. The cards were collected by the staff at the end of each week and served as a complete record of the patients' earnings and spendings during that week.

One use of the token system was as a means of bringing about changes in the treatment program. For example, it was found that patients were spending far too much time in nonsocial activities such as looking at magazines, smoking alone, and solitary recreations. To change this state of affairs, the staff first made available to the patients ongoing opportunities to learn new adaptive social behaviors by developing an ongoing series of structured workshops. These workshops involved activities such as assertiveness training which required frequent and active social interaction. The rates in the token economy were then revised to make participation in the workshop the most highly paid activity. Participation was defined to include active verbal give-and-take in the workshops plus completion of structured homework assignments. As expected, these changes led rather quickly to major increases in social behavior by the patients. The fact that the program had a built-in requirement of practicing the behaviors in settings outside the workshop ensured that the patients would indeed gain experience in trying them out in interpersonal situations which arose in their daily living.

## Mental Retardation

Behavioral psychologists who have worked in residential centers for the mentally retarded frequently draw attention to the astonishing changes that behavior modification procedures have brought about in these settings. In the preface to their edited book on mental retardation, psychologists Travis Thompson and John Grabowski describe conditions which existed in 1968 in one building of the state institution in which they worked. Such conditions have often been so shameful that readers find them difficult to believe. In this particular building of 67 residents, feces were smeared over the floor and the bodies of numerous residents, many of whom were partly or completely naked. Some were huddled in the fetal position, while others walked, ran, or twirled around the room. Most were scarred with recent wounds, and one bled openly. The noise level and the stench were simply unbelievable.

Thompson and Grabowski report that through the use of behavioral technology it was possible to change the conditions over a two-year period into an educational-therapeutic environment. Nowadays, it is the formal policy of many states to drastically limit admission of mentally retarded persons to institutions and instead to develop programs for them in their local communities, so that as many as possible of them can live at home. Nevertheless, many large institutions still exist, and while the grossly inhuman conditions described above will hopefully become a relic of the past, there is still an active need for the application of behavioral principles in these settings. Since the reader will by now be familiar with the principles, we describe applications that are specific to retarded persons.

The behavior of mentally retarded persons differs from that of normal persons in two major ways. First, there is much less variety of behavior. For example, there is much less language. Persons with milder degrees of retardation tend to speak in a normal manner, but they know far fewer words than normal persons. At the profoundly retarded end of the dimension, there are few or no words spoken at all. Also, judgment and problem solving skills are considerably less than normal and are poorly coordinated. These difficulties combine to produce a lack of work skills, social and interpersonal behaviors, and in some cases basic self-care skills.

The second difference is that much of the behavior of mentally retarded persons is socially inappropriate. A mentally retarded child might eat, in addition to food, string, sticks, and feces. He may eliminate in his pants or on the floor. His attention-seeking behavior might involve beating his head against the wall or shrieking at the top of his voice.

The goals of psychoeducational programs for the mentally retarded are to increase the amount of behavior such people are able to display, and to get all this behavior to occur appropriately. To accomplish these ends, researchers now agree that a combination of instructions, demonstrations, physical guidance, and reinforcement procedures have been applied successfully to a wide variety of tasks. In regard to academic learning, significant steps have been made in teaching classroom related behavior such as attending, but there has been relatively little progress in increasing the amount of academic material, such as arithmetic, that is actually learned. Thus, one important avenue for future research could involve an analysis of academic skills into their component parts, and the construction of learning programs to teach each component in turn.

The technique of simple positive reinforcement is ideally suited for teaching many of the behaviors that retarded persons need to learn. Its advantages include the fact that language skills are not required, it can be used by nonprofessional staff after specific training, it can be applied to any behavior with no special preparation on the child's part, and it can also be used for eliminating undesired behavior. Two related basic principles are also important. One is *shaping*, the use of successive approximations or small steps, which was introduced in Chapter 2. Shaping is particularly important with retarded persons because the amount of new learning which they can grasp at one step is generally small. Thus it may be necessary to use more steps in teaching a simple task to a retarded child than to a normal child. The second important principle is *chaining*, a technique for teaching complex sequences of behaviors such as dressing, to be described below.

Because the teaching of mentally retarded persons is more lengthy and difficult than normal persons, behavioral technologists have been challenged to discover more efficient and effective ways of applying the principles of learning in teaching everyday skills. We illustrate some of these procedures with reference to specific areas of skills training in children.

### Dressing

Everyday tasks like dressing, learned readily by normal children, are complex and overwhelming tasks for the retarded. Psychologist

Luke Watson has provided the following detailed description of a stepwise procedure for teaching a child to put on a short-sleeved pullover shirt. He has divided the task into five basic steps.

In order to teach the child to regard the end of one step as a cue to begin the next step, training starts with the final step of the sequence. Thus, the child is shown how to pull the hem of the shirt down from the rib cage to the waist position. As soon as he has done so, he is reinforced with social approval plus tangible reinforcement such as food. When the child has mastered this step, the shirt is put on him only as far as one arm into the sleeve hole. He is then instructed or shown how to put his other arm into the sleeve hole, and this is followed by the task he has already learned, namely, pulling the shirt band down to the waist. Reinforcement follows immediately as before.

When these two steps have been mastered and are regularly being performed together, the shirt is simply pulled down over the child's back and he is shown how to put the first arm into the arm hole. He is then instructed to follow it with the two behaviors already learned, and is reinforced for the complete package as before. In the fourth step, the shirt is placed on top of the child's head, and he begins by pulling it down over his head. In the fifth step, the trainer simply hands the shirt to the child, who engages in all five steps before being reinforced.

The child must be permitted to proceed at his own pace, and the number of specific steps required will vary from child to child. The child himself directs the learning by his success or lack of success; if he does not master the task, he is directing the trainer to change the procedure. Verbal reinforcement and prompts can be used throughout the process. As the child engages in more of the behavior, the prompts can be faded and then eliminated altogether.

Chaining refers to a procedure in which a number of complex behavioral units, such as putting on separate garments, are taught in a sequence. Thus, the child might be taught the individual skills of putting on different garments, and then these are chained together by using the same procedure as described for a single garment. The trainer might begin the procedure by separately instructing the child to put on all individual items except shoes. At the words "get dressed," the child would be instructed to put his shoes on and would be reinforced for doing so. For the second step, "get dressed" would be the signal for putting on first the socks and then the shoes. Finally, the child would be taught to respond to "get dressed" from a naked state and to put on all garments in their correct order.

Toilet Training

Toilet training for the retarded is an area in which rapid advances have recently been made. Some behavioral psychologists now believe that it is possible to toilet train even the most profoundly retarded individuals, and that further technical developments in this area will involve refining the procedures and developing techniques for maintaining the behavior on a stable basis. Two different procedures have been devised for toilet training retarded persons. Both can, of course, be applied to normal children. The impetus for developing and refining them has come from the need to deal with the lack of bowel and bladder control as major problems in traditional institutions for the retarded.

The first procedure is similar to what is used by most parents of normal children. The child is taken to the toilet at times when he is most likely to eliminate and is rewarded with praise and/or food and other reinforcers for success. Psychologists Richard Foxx and Nathan Azrin have recently refined this procedure into a short term intensive training package. The child is given a large quantity of liquids, and may be seated on the toilet for as much as five hours out of an eight hour training period. An electrical device in the bottom of the toilet chair signals when urination or defecation has occurred, and immediate reinforcement is given. Reinforcement is also given at five-minute intervals if the child remains dry. Accidents are treated by having the child undress, wash the soiled area, and then wash the soiled clothing. This procedure has been reported to be successful with most retarded persons within two weeks. The reader will appreciate, however, that it is both time-consuming and quite aversive for the staff to carry out.

The second method, developed by psychologist Keith Van Wagenen, uses training pants containing a moisture sensitive device which sounds a tone whenever the pants are wet. At the tone, the training person shouts "No," and quickly takes the child to the toilet for the remainder of the urination. After a number of trials, the use of the training person is gradually faded out, and the child learns to go directly to the toilet when the tone sounds. A possibly more effective procedure is to begin the entire training sequence by first teaching the child to respond to the sound of the tone by going to the toilet, lowering his pants, and preparing to eliminate.

It should be emphasized that these procedures are for day-time toilet training, and while for most normal children daytime bowel and bladder control will soon lead automatically to control during the night, there are often exceptions. The best-known procedure for controlling nocturnal urination in both normal and retarded children is the pad-and-bell system, developed as long ago as 1938 by psychologists O. Hobart Mowrer and W. M. Mowrer. In this method, the device is placed on the mattress under the bottom sheet, and wetness completes an electrical circuit, causing a bell to ring. As training progresses, the child is awakened progressively earlier and earlier in the urination. Another procedure, which could be used in conjunction with the bell-and-pad, is simply to have the child report during the day whenever he needs to urinate, and then to have him wait, first for short periods, and then for progressively longer and longer periods, before actually doing so.

There are many other areas in which behavioral technology has made a profound difference to the behavior and lives of mentally retarded persons and those who care for them. Some of the major areas which we have not mentioned include eating behavior, social skills, aggressive behavior, self-injurious behavior, and vocational skills. It is anticipated that in the future there will be further developments in these and other areas of importance to the mentally retarded.

## Juvenile Delinquency

The treatment of adolescents with chronic and persistent antisocial behavior has traditionally been a difficult and unrewarding task. While this area remains a problem for society, the use of behavioral procedures has resulted in some highly significant improvements in the effectiveness of treatment within the past ten or fifteen years. Before we proceed to describe these programs, it is important for the reader to understand that the term "behavior modification" has been loosely applied to a number of ethically questionable, highly coercive procedures in penal institutions, procedures which have nothing at all to do with the behavioral technology developed by psychologists and described in this book. Unfortunately, these questionable programs have received a great deal of publicity and political attention, seriously hampering the appropriate and beneficial uses of behavioral technology in the design of prison rehabilitation programs. Nevertheless, applications to so-called delinquent behaviors have made some very significant advances. It is important to recognize that we are talking not about a particular class of *people*, but about a class of *behavior*. In other words, behavioral psychologists who work with juvenile delinquents deemphasize the notion that delinquency is a personality characteristic, and emphasize that they are dealing with adolescents who happen to exhibit certain kinds of behaviors.

Behavioral technology has been applied to juvenile treatment programs of two kinds: institutional settings, and small-group residential programs in community settings. We describe each of these applications in turn.

## Institutional Programs

We have already discussed the use of behavioral procedures in institutional programs for long-term psychiatric patients and for mentally retarded persons. Their use in institutions for delinquent adolescents is similar in basic structure. The first step is to specify those behaviors which need to be increased and those which need to be decreased. The second is to develop a special environment in which expectations are made clear to the residents, cues for appropriate behavior are provided, and a reinforcement system is implemented. The system generally involves the use of tokens, backed up by primary reinforcers.

Although token economy programs have indeed been able to produce meaningful changes, they suffer from several disadvantages. One is that material reinforcers are much more powerful for delinquent adolescents than social reinforcers such as praise, approval, or recognition. Thus there is the problem that once the tokens and the back-up reinforcers are withdrawn, behavior begins to deteriorate. Another disadvantage is shared by other institutional programs that we have described, namely, that the practice of isolating socially deviant people in large institutions away from their homes is not an effective procedure for bringing about meaningful changes. As we have seen, this practice is nowadays being discontinued whenever possible in favor of small group living facilities based in the person's local community.

A key component of the difficulty of bringing about lasting changes in residents of institutions is that the changes are often not maintained when the residents are returned to their own communities. The reason is that they are confronted once again with the original cues that triggered the delinquent or other deviant behavior in the first place. At the very least, therefore, a parallel effort must be made to change the behavior of the individual's parents, peers, teachers, etc. A serious problem for those mental health professionals who wish to de-emphasize large scale institutional treatment, however, is that there is often considerable pressure from local community officials, as well as parents and teachers, to get delinquent adolescents out of the community. Parallel to this pressure is the frequent community resistance to establishing small-group treatment centers in the community. These are continuing issues in local politics and will probably be so for some time to come.

## Community Residential Programs

It is in small group residential programs that behavioral procedures have made their most significant contributions to the treatment of juvenile delinquency. Despite the opposition mentioned above, the growth of these programs has been extremely rapid in the last few years as entire states have converted their juvenile correction systems from the large-scale institutional model to small community-based facilities. A most important advantage of these programs is that their environments are similar in two major ways to the adolescent's home environment. First, the small group living situations are built around small family units, so that the day-to-day cooperative living behaviors required of the residents are similar to those in a regular home. Second, because the adolescents are living in their own communities, the counselors are able to have them focus on the actual ongoing problems that are significant for their community adjustment, problems such as their schoolwork, peer relationships, relationships with their parents, and job aspirations and training.

An outstanding example of a community-based residential program for delinquent adolescents is Achievement Place in Lawrence,

Kansas, which was developed initially by psychologists Elery and Elaine Philips. In the Achievement Place model, of which there are now a number of similar homes in several states, the home houses six to eight adolescents ranging from 12 to 16 years of age. Also present are two "teaching parents," who manage the overall program and act as behavior change agents. The program provides a highly structured environment with modeling and reinforcement for those behaviors and values that are reinforced in the local community, such as cooperativeness, academic achievement, and taking responsibility. Behaviors that would be inappropriate in the community, such as lying, stealing, and fighting, are systematically punished. The basic system of reinforcement and punishment involves a point system or token economy. Residents record the points they earn on a card, and newly entering residents can exchange their points each day for privileges. When a resident has fully learned the connection between points and privileges, the exchange for privileges is delayed to once a week. For the most advanced residents, the point system is done away with altogether in favor of a merit system in which privileges are free. Residents must progress satisfactorily through the merit system before being permitted to return to their own homes.

There are almost 200 different behaviors in the treatment program for which points can be earned at some time or other. Privileges which can be purchased with points are also highly varied, and include the following six categories: basics, such as the use of tools and going outside; snacks; time away to go home or downtown; weekly allowance of one to three dollars; savings bonds for special purposes such as clothes; and other special privileges. As already stated, the basic emphasis of the program is on teaching the residents appropriate behaviors that are needed for successful participation in the community. Residents must be able to function on the merit system before being transferred to their natural homes, and the teaching parents work with each resident's natural parents or guardians to help them devise a reinforcement system to help maintain the behaviors learned at Achievement Place.

A substantial amount of careful research has been conducted on the procedures employed at Achievement Place, and it has clearly demonstrated that the procedures are effective in bringing about the desired behavioral changes. Most recently, increasing emphasis has been given to the modification of social behavior, and positive results in this area have also been reported. Another recent development has been the use of the residents themselves in the administration of the Achievement Place system. This has provided an excellent demonstration that the residents can indeed accept administrative responsibilities; in fact, they appear to function better in some ways under such a system.

## Behavior Change Systems in the Classroom

In Chapter 8 we described the use of behavioral procedures to deal constructively with problems which individual children may experience, with the therapist working either through the parents in the home setting or the teacher in the classroom. In addition to the application of individual behavior therapy procedures, many teachers have implemented classroom systems for managing both normal and problem behaviors, usually with the collaboration of a psychologist consultant. Let us look at the characteristics of these systems and the ways in which they are utilized to promote and maintain desired behaviors.

Behavior management systems in the classroom have usually involved points or tokens. The philosophy of their use, and their advantages and disadvantages, are similar to those we have described above in regard to psychiatric patients. There are several particular advantages to a token system as a way of motivating behavior in the classroom. First, children will usually work for tokens if there is a variety of attractive back-up reinforcers. Second, some difficult or disruptive children who are unresponsive to social reinforcement will respond to tokens. Third, tokens alert children to response-consequence relationships and thus enhance the learning of self-control.

Initiating the use of tokens as reinforcers in a classroom setting involves the same procedural steps as we have described previously. However, the following should be especially noted. First, it is most important to specify clearly the behaviors for which tokens can be earned, preferably in writing and in the constant view of the students. Likewise, the rules by which tokens are to be awarded should be clear to the students and should also be written down or else frequently reviewed with them. Third, the children should be explicitly and thoroughly informed of the exact nature of the back-up reinforcers that the tokens will buy, and also the exact times at which the exchange can take place.

It is often desirable to permit children to choose from a list, or "menu," of back-up rewards, all of which have been selected to have some specific value. A wide variety of possible back-up reinforcers is available, and for the enterprising teacher the list can be almost endless. Rewards can be tangible, such as comics, small plastic rings, baseball cards, or slogan buttons. They can involve the use of facilities or privileges, such as use of the typewriter, access to the swimming pool, wearing the teacher's sunglasses, or putting up one's own poster for the day. They can involve special but limited activities, such as feeding the class hamster, stage managing the class play, or correcting papers. Literally anything that has value for the children can be offered as a back-up reinforcer. They can also include brief access to activities that would normally be taboo to the children, such as chewing gum in class, putting one's head on the desk, or going to the drinking fountain without permission.

The above list is not meant to play down the importance of social rewards. However, teacher approval and warmth must be applied at the right time, and for some children approval will not be sufficient to get initial changes started.

Reinforcers tend to be more effective if they are not readily available from elsewhere. Also, they should be a natural part of the educational setting. Because children will tire of the same reinforcers after a time, it is advisable to have an adequate variety available and to add new ones periodically. The children should, of course, be immediately and fully informed of the changes. For reinforcers that are to be consumed by the children right in the classroom while other children are doing something else, the program is enhanced if an area is designated for reinforcement that is separate from the task area. Another way of improving the effectiveness of a token system is to keep written records in full view of the students; for example, charts of the number of tokens that have been earned for different activities, and of the number of tokens that each child has spent. Because it is important for all children to have success and mastery experiences, the records should be of behaviors that are within the capability of all students.

There have recently been criticisms of token reinforcement systems in school settings, some by psychologists themselves. It is argued, for example, that behavior modification programs are more often than not geared to making children quiet and docile, conforming to the teacher's needs. Whether the children learn anything, it is claimed, tends to be ignored in favor of a preoccupation with producing orderly and well-behaved conformists. Such critics often favor the opposite type of environment, the "open" or "free" classroom, in which children select their own learning materials and traditional rules of discipline are relaxed. Open environments have themselves been criticized, however, as ineffective for adequate learning, particularly for children with academic and social problems.

The availability of a sophisticated technology of learning and behavior change now enables teachers and administrators to design a system to produce just about any kind of person they want. Thus, there is a growing need for extensive dialogue and planning among educators and the general public in order to decide what kinds of qualities and characteristics we want our children to have now and as adults. Schools are becoming more and more in a position to assist in the development of these characteristics, and it is most important that the general public maintain an active interest in the future of their children.

# Epilogue: Toward the Future

What does the future hold for behavior therapy, for the application of the principles of behavior to the treatment of psychological disorders and the solution of other human difficulties? Most behavior therapists believe that the answer to this question depends basically on the new knowledge that researchers will be able to discover about human behavior and ways of changing it. The interested reader will find a wide variety of research-oriented textbooks available on behavior therapy. A recent example is Harold Leitenberg's edited *Handbook of Behavior Modification and Behavior Therapy*. In addition, the journal *Behavior Therapy* is a major publication source for research in behavior therapy.

Besides research, several other influences will be important in shaping the future of behavior therapy. One centers on current and future trends in the way in which mental health services are provided in our society. Another involves common criticisms of behavior therapy and their implications for the future of the field. A third is the rapidly increasing array of behavior-change packages that are becoming available to the general public.

## Provision of Mental Health Services

Who will be the providers of behavior change services in the future? The technology for human change that has been developed by behavioral scientists is gradually being disseminated throughout the mental health professions and is becoming available to all who are concerned with helping others to make personal changes that improve the quality of their lives. Parallel to this development is an influx of new personnel into the human services field. Most of today's "primary-care givers" are not doctoral-level persons, but are teachers, nurses, ministers, counselors for specific areas such as drug problems, alcoholism, marriage, and child abuse, and many other persons whose formal education might be at the masters, bachelors, or high school level. Some of these persons are trained comprehensively, while others receive on-the-job training in the specific techniques of behavior change that are needed for their particular roles. Ongoing consultation and supervision is provided by persons who have more extensive and comprehensive training in the technology of behavior change. In this regard, a recent major breakthrough in the delivery of mental health services to low-income and minority groups has been the discovery that a vital role is played by personnel from the same minority group or low-income community.

## Common Criticisms of Behavior Therapy

"Deep" versus "superficial" treatment. A common criticism of behavior therapy procedures has been that they bring about only superficial changes in the person's difficulties, enough to show some temporary improvement, perhaps, but not enough to really affect the basic causes and therefore ensure lasting change.

This criticism reflects a sharp difference of opinion among mental health professionals on a very fundamental issue, involving both the causes of disordered behavior and the principles underlying its treatment. One position on this issue involves the "disease" or "medical" model of psychological disorder, so called because it holds that psychological disorders are the same in principle as physical or medical disorders. In this view, psychological disorders are best regarded as diseases, analogous to physical diseases. Each disease has a distinct cause, sometimes physical, and it is important, if not essential, to determine the cause in order to make a diagnosis and select the correct treatment. The most meaningful material for purposes of psychological diagnosis and treatment is said to be the deepest or most unconscious, and generally involves early childhood experiences. Any other approach is regarded as superficial and insufficient.

Behavioral psychologists do not share this view. Research evidence shows that early childhood experiences are often not significant in the development and treatment of a problem, although at times they may be. Nor is it always necessary to know the circumstances surrounding the initial development of the problem. In some cases, of course, this information will indeed be of considerable help, although behaviorally oriented treatment does not necessarily deal with these original conditions. Thus, the conceptualization and treatment of a psychological problem does not have to be "deep," in the sense described above, in order to be successful.

The science of behavior has now developed to the point where it is clear that the principles of the "mind" are not an extension of the principles of the body, but are different, and require a separate science. Having made this distinction between biological science and behavioral science, we should also point out that there are many disorders to which both sciences contribute significantly. In fact, some of the most interesting areas about which little is known at the present time involve the interaction between biology and behavior.

**Symptom substitution.** We have described the basic concern stemming from the disease or medical model, namely, that behavioral treatment is, by its very nature, ineffective. If a person's complaints are merely symptoms of a basic underlying disease, and if the therapist attends only to the symptoms without identifying and treating the underlying disease, then new symptoms will soon substitute for those that have been removed. Researchers in behavior therapy have taken this criticism seriously, and the research results to date have clearly demonstrated that new "symptoms" rarely occur. In studies of the treatment of interpersonal anxieties, for example, clients' overall level of adjustment has been shown to improve in the year or two following treatment.

Some instances have occurred in behavioral treatment where a new problem has emerged to substitute for the old. The behavior therapist would regard this outcome as a failure on his part to teach the needed adaptive behaviors to the person before helping him to eliminate the old unadaptive behaviors. The therapist is most certainly concerned with the new behavior that occurs after the undesired behavior is eliminated, and actively engages the patient in deciding what new behaviors will be arranged to substitute for the old ones. From this viewpoint, the word "symptom" is simply a label that is applied if the new behavior should happen to be an undersirable one, and such an outcome would signify poor planning by the behavior therapist.

**Is behavior therapy coercive?** As stated in Chapter 9, perhaps the most extensive and constant criticism leveled at behavior therapy procedures is that they are unduly coercive and therefore unethical. This criticism has taken a number of different forms, one of which has involved the penal system. After token economy programs were found to be helpful in long-term psychiatric settings and other institutional settings, there was interest in getting similar results in prison settings. Unfortunately, most of the programs that were set up in prisons bore little resemblance to an adequately designed system based on behavioral science. Rather, the term "behavior modification" was used as an excuse for unreasonable procedures involving physical abuse and other unethical practices. The ensuing public criticism dragged the term behavior modification into disrepute, and indiscriminately linked it with psychosurgery and the use of electric shock for punishment purposes. As a result, the term behavior modification is now used sparingly by behavioral psychologists, and the potential benefits to the penal system from the application of ethical and well-designed behavioral programs are still some years away.

It is interesting to note that the public at large seems extremely reluctant to acknowledge that active control of human behavior occurs at all in our society. Most people appear to believe and fear that any control is automatically bad. The truth is, of course, that behavioral principles can be used for both good and bad purposes, and have been freely used in both ways for thousands of years. Because these principles are now organized and formalized into a structured system as part of a scientific discipline, the fact of their active use can no longer be ignored. "Good" uses have included successful child-rearing practices, religious instruction, the development and operation of the legal system, and the advertising industry. "Bad" uses include "brainwashing" in prisoner-of-war camps, propaganda by political factions other than your own, and the threat of excessive government controls, as exemplified in George Orwell's novel *Nineteen Eighty-four*. It should thus be perfectly clear that the issue of using behavioral principles is not a scientific one, but is simply a fact of life. Monitoring the use of behavioral principles has always been, and should continue to be, a matter of broad social responsibility. Because behavioral scientists have played a major part in formalizing and publicizing the existence and use of these principles, however, they should also take a major share of the responsibility for their appropriate social use.

## Behavior Change for the Consumer

Behavior change procedures are now beginning to join the list of do-it-yourself packages that are available to the public outside the mainstream of the mental health and human service industry. Examples can be seen in the development of commercially based services for weight control and for quitting smoking. Many of these programs are based upon sound behavioral technology, and offer comprehensive packages of assistance at competitive prices. Behaviorally oriented treatment groups are also becoming popular in areas such as assertiveness training and stress management, and a steady stream of behavioral self-help books is appearing on these and other topics.

How effective are these programs and remedies? By now the reader should have developed a respectful appreciation for the complexity of behavioral technology, and for the great many pieces of information that must be considered and questions that must be answered before behavior change technology can be successfully applied to any given case. We have also seen that the problem for which a person seeks help is sometimes not the problem which must be approached first in order to bring about the desired changes. Thus, we would predict that only a minority of persons, whose problems are simple and straightforward, would be likely to benefit significantly from commercial and self-help programs.

We do not mean to imply that the popular literature on behavior change procedures is of little value. On the contrary, it provides an interesting and personally absorbing way for people to become familiar with behaviorally oriented procedures for human change. And public education is a basic and necessary step in enabling society to take full advantage of any field of endeavor.

What about group programs in weight control, assertiveness training, quitting smoking, anxiety management, and the like? Potential consumers should realize that the existence of these programs often depends on the profit motive, and should "do their homework" before making a purchase of services. It should also be recognized that even the best of groups cannot cure all ills, and that uncomplicated problems are easier to treat than complicated ones. Perhaps the soundest approach to evaluating the worth of a behavior change service of any kind is to make inquiries about the professional training and affiliations of the person in charge. Two basic avenues for making such inquiries are through the psychology department of your local university or college, and the national organization of professionals interested in behavior therapy, the Association for the Advancement of Behavior Therapy, at 420 Lexington Avenue, New York, NY 10017.

Obviously, no amount of prior information can offer an absolute guarantee, and the question of consumer protection is likely to become increasingly important as the availability of such services becomes more widespread. However, the probability of receiving positive benefit from a behavioral program can be increased by first seeking the advice of people who are likely to be best informed on the topic.

# References

Atthowe, J. M., Jr. (1976). Treating the hospitalized person. In W. E. Craighead, A. E. Kazdin, and M. J. Mahoney (eds.), *Behavior modification: Principles, Issues, and Applications*. Boston: Houghton Mifflin.

Ayllon, T. (1965). Some behavioral problems associated with eating in chronic schizophrenic patients. In L. P. Ullmann and L. Krasner (eds.), *Case Studies in Behavior Modification*. New York: Holt, Rinehart, and Winston.

Azrin, N. H., and R. M. Foxx (1973). *Toilet Training in Less Than a Day*. New York: Pergamon.

Bach, G. R., and P. Wyden (1968). *The Intimate Enemy*. New York: Avon.

Bandura, A. (ed.) (1971). *Psychological Modeling*. Chicago: Aldine/Atherton.

Briddell, D. W., and P. E. Nathan (1976). Behavior assessment and modification with alcoholics. In M. Hersen, R. M. Eisler, and P. M. Miller (eds.), *Progress in Behavior Modification*, Vol. 2. New York: Academic Press.

Britt, M. F. (1975). *Bibliography of Behavior Modification 1924–1975*. Durham, N.C.: Cerebral Palsy and Crippled Children's Hospital of North Carolina.

Craighead, W. E., A. E. Kazdin, and M. J. Mahoney (1976). *Behavior Modification: Principles, Issues, and Applications*. Boston: Houghton Mifflin.

Ellis, A. (1962). *Reason and Emotion in Psychotherapy*. New York: Lyle Stuart.

Fordyce, W. E. (1976). *Behavioral Methods for Chronic Pain and Illness.* St. Louis: Mosby.

Fuchs, C. Z., and L. P. Rehm (1977). A self-control behavior therapy program for depression. *Journal of Consulting and Clinical Psychology* 45, 206–215.

Goldstein, S. B., and R. I. Lanyon (1971). Patient therapists in the language training of an autistic child. *Journal of Speech and Hearing Disorders* 36, 552–560.

Jackson, B. (1972). Treatment of depression by self-reinforcement. *Behavior Therapy* 3, 298–307.

Jacobson, E. (1929). *Progressive Relaxation.* Chicago: University of Chicago Press.

Kazdin, A. E., and R. R. Bootzin (1972). The token economy: An evaluative review. *Journal of Applied Behavior Analysis* 5, 343–372.

Khan, A. U., C. Bonk, and Y. Gordon (1974). Non-allergic asthma and process. *Annals of Allergy* 32, 245–251.

Kinsey, A. C., W. B. Pomeroy, and C. E. Martin (1948). *Sexual Behavior in the Human Male.* Philadelphia: Saunders.

Kinsey, A. C., W. B. Pomeroy, C. E. Martin, and P. H. Gebhart (1953). *Sexual Behavior in the Human Female.* Philadelphia: Saunders.

Lange, A. J., and P. Jakubowski (1976). *Responsible Assertive Behavior.* Champaign, Ill.: Research Press.

Lanyon, R. I., and B. P. Lanyon (1976). Behavioral assessment and decision-making: the design of strategies for therapeutic behavior change. In M. P. Feldman and A. Broadhurst (eds.), *Theoretical and Experimental Bases of the Behavior Therapies.* London/New York: Wiley.

Leitenberg, H. (ed.) (1976). *Handbook of Behavior Modification and Behavior Therapy.* Englewood Cliffs, N.J.: Prentice-Hall.

Liberman, R. P., L. W. King, and W. J. DeRisi (1976). Behavior analysis and therapy in community mental health. In H. Leitenberg (ed.), *Handbook of Behavior Modification and Behavior Therapy.* Englewood Cliffs, N. J.: Prentice-Hall.

Lloyd, R. W., and H. C. Salzberg (1975). Controlled social drinking: an alternative to abstinence as a treatment goal for some alcohol abusers. *Psychological Bulletin* 82, 815–842.

Mahoney, M. J., and K. Mahoney (1976). *Permanent Weight Control.* New York: Norton.

Masters, W. H., and V. Johnson (1970). *Human Sexual Inadequacy.* Boston: Little, Brown.

Masters, W. H., and V. Johnson (1966). *Human Sexual Response.* Boston: Little, Brown.

Meichenbaum, D. H. (1977). *Cognitive-Behavior Modification*. New York: Plenum.

Mowrer, O. H., and W. M. Mowrer (1938). Enuresis: A method for its study and treatment. *American Journal of Orthopsychiatry* 8, 436–439.

O'Leary, S. G., and K. D. O'Leary (1976). Behavior modification in the school. In H. Leitenberg (ed.), *Handbook of Behavior Modification and Behavior Therapy*. Englewood Cliffs, N. J.: Prentice-Hall.

Patterson, G. R., and M. E. Gullion (1968). *Living with Children*. Champaign, Ill.: Research Press.

Phillips, E. L., E. A. Phillips, D. L. Fixsen, and M. M. Wolf (1971). Achievement Place: Modification of the behavior of pre-delinquent boys within a token economy. *Journal of Applied Behavior Analysis* 4, 45–59.

Seligman, M. E. P., and S. F. Maier (1976). Learned helplessness: Theory and evidence. *Journal of Experimental Psychology: General* 105, 3–46.

Stuart, R. B., and B. Davis (1972). *Slim Chance in a Fat World*. Champaign, Ill.: Research Press.

Tharp, R. G., D. C. Watson, and J. Kaya (1974). Self-modification of depression. *Journal of Consulting and Clinical Psychology* 42, 624.

Thompson, T., and J. Grabowski (eds.) (1972). *Behavior Modification of the Mentally Retarded*. New York: Oxford University Press.

Thoreson, C. E., and M. J. Mahoney (1974). *Behavioral Self-Control*. New York: Holt, Rinehart, and Winston.

Van Wagenen, R. K., L. Meyerson, N. J. Kerr, and K. Mahoney (1969). Field Trials of a new procedure for toilet training. *Journal of Experimental Child Psychology* 8, 147–159.

Watson, L. J. (1973). *Child Behavior Modification*. New York: Pergamon.

Winett, R. A., and R. C. Winkler (1972). Current behavior modification in the classroom: be still, be quite, be docile. *Journal of Applied Behavior Analysis* 5, 499–504.

Wolpe, J. (1958). *Psychotherapy by Reciprocal Inhibition*. Stanford, Calif.: Stanford University Press.

Wolpe, J. (1976) *Theme and Variations: A Behavior Therapy Casebook*. New York: Pergamon.

Zigler, E., and L. Phillips (1962). Social Competence and the process-reactive distinction in schizophrenia. *Journal of Abnormal and Social Psychology* 65, 215–222.

# Index

Achievement Place, 174-176
Acting-out, 100-102
Adaptive self-statements, *see* Self-statements, positive
Addiction, definition of, 103
Aggressive behavior, 89
Alcoholism, 28-29, 103-105
Alone, fear of being, 12, 19-20, 44-45
Anger, expressing, 51-52, 57-58, 100-102
Antabuse, 28
Anxiety, 16, 66-78
  causes of, 67
  and cognitive interference, 69
  physiological aspects of, 69
  treatment of, 70-82
Apathy, *see* Meaninglessness
Articulation, speech, 145-155
Assertiveness training, 54-57, 88-94
Assessment, 9-21, 51-52, 113-114, 121-122, 145-147, 149-150
Association for the Advancement of Behavior Therapy, 184
Asthma, 79, 82
Atthowe, John, 165
Autism, 145-155
Aversive imagery, 105, 114, 117-119
Aversive procedures, 159-160
Ayllon, Teodoro, 162
Azrin, Nathan, 171

Bach, George, 58
Back-up reinforcers, 157, 163, 165, 166, 176
Bandura, Albert, 37–38
Behavior, definition of, 3
  involuntary, 7
  rehearsal, 91, 96–97
  voluntary, 7
Biofeedback, 70, 81–82

Chaining, 170
Change agents, 25–26
Child molesting, 115–118
Childbirth, natural, 139–140
Children, 141–160
Chronic patients, 162–166
Classroom behavior, 157–159, 176–178
Clinical skills, 9
Cognitive difficulties, treating, 77–78
Cognitive learning, 34–37
Cognitive restructuring, 36
Communication, improving, 58–59
Community mental health, 94, 166–167
Consultation, 141–178
Contract, behavioral, 132
  therapeutic, 2, 10, 13–14
Contracting, contingency, 156–157
Control of behavior, 182–183
Conversational skills, 98, 117
Coué, Emile, 34
Counterconditioning, 71
Covert events, 3
Criticisms, 180–183
Cues, 4–5, 34
  discovering, 71–72

Dating, 95–102
Davis, B., 18
Death, fear of, 49, 59–61
"Deep" versus "superficial" treatment, 180–181
Delinquency, 172–176
Dependency, 12
Depression, 82–86
  post-partum, 50
  self-management of, 136–137

Desensitization, 39–40, 61, 70–75, 95–96, 109, 139
Determinism, 3
Discrimination training, 34
Dressing, 169–171

Ejaculatory incompetence, 112
Ellis, Albert, 36, 134
Empathy, 9
Encopresis, 144
Epilepsy, 82
Ethics, 182–183
Exhibitionism, 115–119
Existential dilemma, 13
Existential philosophy, 3
Extinction, 33, 71

Family therapy, 143
Fears, 47–66
Feedback, 30, 31
Fingernail biting, 130–131
"Flooding," 41, 73
Fordyce, Wilbert, 137–138
Foxx, Richard, 171
Free will, 3
Freud, Sigmund, 1, 108, 159
Frigidity, 109–112

Goal-setting, 31–32
Grabowski, John, 168
Gullion, M. Elizabeth, 147

Headaches, migraine, 82
  tension, 76, 79–82
Hierarchy, 31, 41, 44, 55–56, 74
Homework assignments, 24, 30
Homosexuality, 97–101, 112–115
Hypertension, 82
Hypnosis, 38
Hysteria, 79

Imagery, 26, 32, 75, 95–96, 105
  training, 38–41
Imaginal learning, 38–41
Implosion, 73
Impotence, 109–111
Impulsive behavior, 100–102, 158
Insight, 25
Insomnia, 6, 7

Index 191

Interpersonal skills, 87–105, 163
Irrational beliefs, changing, 61–62

Jackson, Barry, 136
Jacobson, Edmund, 75
Jakubowski, Patricia, 89
Johnson, Virginia, 42, 107–112

Kinsey, Alfred, 108–109

Lamaze, Fernand, 139
Lange, Arthur, 89
Learned helplessness, 84
Learning, cognitive, 34–37
  principles of, 30–32
  procedures for, 32–46
Liberman, Robert, 166

Mahoney, Michael, 18
Mahoney, Kathryn, 18
Maintenance of behavior, 127, 174
Marital problems, 49, 120–125
Masculine behaviors, 97, 99–101
Masters, William, 42, 107–112
Meaninglessness, 12–13, 20–21, 45–46
Medical model, 23, 181
Medical problems, comparison with, 23
Meichenbaum, Donald, 135–136
Mental health services, 180
Mental retardation, 167–172
MMPI, 11, 51, 146
Modeling, 37–38, 95, 100–101, 109, 152–155
  imaginal, 40
Motivation, 13
Mowrer, O. Hobart, 172

Negative self-statements, 134

Obesity, 6, 10–11, 17–18, 42–44
Observation, 14–21
Observational learning, see Modeling
Obsessional fears, 47–66
Obsessional thoughts, 36
Orgasmic dysfunction, 109–112

Pain, chronic, 82, 137–138
Parent training, 141–160
Patterson, Gerald, 147
Pedophilia, see child molesting
Phillips, Elaine, 175
Phillips, Elery, 175
Phillips, Leslie, 88
Physical problems, 78–81
Pleasant events, 26
Practice, 30, 95
Premature ejaculation, 112
Problem, definition of, 6
Psychiatric hospitals, 161–162
Psychoanalysis, 8
Psychosomatic problems, 78–81
Psychosurgery, 182
Psychotherapy, relationship, 8
Public speaking, fear of, 39
Punishment, 32–34

Rage, 51
Record-keeping, 14–21, 59, 149–150
Rehearsal, 30, 45, 109
  cognitive, 35
  imaginal, 40
Rehm, Lynn, 136
Reinforcement, 32–34, 44, 152–155, 176
  principle of, 4
Reinforcers, 26
  removing, 71
Relationship, therapeutic, 7–8
Relaxation, muscle, 39, 75–77, 140
Research, 179–182
Resources for treatment, 24–27
Rights, human, 90–91
Rogers, Carl, 1

Self-administered consequences, 132–134
Self-help programs, 183–184
Self-help skills, 163
Self-image, 53
Self-management, 41–42, 126–140
Self-observation, 15–16, 24, 54, 59, 77–78, 129–131
Self-statements, positive, 43, 53, 134
Seligman, Martin, 84
Semans, J. H., 112

Sensate focus, 42
Sexual deviations, 29, 115–119
Sexual problems, 42, 106–125
Shaping, 31, 33, 109
Shyness, 6
Sickness, fear of, 59–61
Smoking, 131
Social drinking, 103–104
Social skills training, 94–101, 117
Stimulus, 4
Stimulus-control, 43, 130–131
Stuart, Frieda, 121
Stuart, Richard, 18, 121
Studying, 131
Stuttering, 82
Successive approximations, 31, 162, see also shaping
Symptom substitution, 28, 181–182

Teacher training, 141–160
Temper, losing one's, 100–102
Tension, 70, 75–76
Tharp, Roland, 137
Thompson, Travis, 168
Thought stopping, 36, 52–53

Thunderstorms, fear of, 73–75
Time-out, 159–160
Toilet training, 171–172
Token economy, 94, 162–166, 173–176
Transference, 8
Transvestism, 115–119
Treatment strategies, designing, 27–32

Ulcers, 82

Vaginal muscles, 140
Vaginismus, 112
Van Wagenen, Keith, 171
Vasocongestion, 109
Voice quality, changing, 100

Watson, Luke, 169–171
Will-power, 126
Wolpe, Joseph, 36, 39
Wyden, Peter, 58

Zigler, Edward, 88